W9-BUH-585

DISCARD

SOUTHEAST ASIA TOMORROW

SOUTHEAST ASIA TOMORROW

Problems and Prospects for US Policy

Melvin Gurtov

The Johns Hopkins Press
Baltimore and London

Copyright © 1970 by The RAND Corporation
All rights reserved
Manufactured in the United States of America

The Johns Hopkins Press, Baltimore, Maryland 21218
The Johns Hopkins Press Ltd., London

Library of Congress Catalog Card Number 79-101457

Standard Book Number 8018-1121-X (clothbound edition)
Standard Book Number 8018-1120-1 (paperback edition)

Originally published, 1970
Johns Hopkins Paperbacks edition, 1970

For Rochelle

CONTENTS

PREFACE   ix

I. INTRODUCTION: THE STRATEGIC ASSESS-
   MENT OF SOUTHEAST ASIA IN 1954 AND
   ITS IMPLICATIONS   1

II. THE SECURITY PICTURE IN SOUTHEAST
    ASIA   7
    Vietnam: The Implications of Withdrawal   7
    The Meaning of Vietnam for Southeast Asia's
       Security   12

III. AMERICAN INTERESTS IN SOUTHEAST ASIA   31
     Approaches to Delineating the National Interest   31
     Vital American Interests in Southeast Asia   34

IV. PROBLEMS AND PROSPECTS FOR US INTER-
    ESTS IN SOUTHEAST ASIA OVER THE NEXT
    TEN YEARS   41
    American Domestic Constraints   41
    The British Withdrawal   42
    Similar Problems of Development in Southeast
       Asian Nations   43
    Communist China   48
    The Soviet Role in Southeast Asia   57
    Japan and Southeast Asia   60

V. TOWARD AN AMERICAN POLICY FOR THE
   NEXT DECADE   63
   Policies Toward Vital Areas of US Interest   64
   Policies Toward Nonvital Areas of US Interest   83

VI. CONCLUSION   101

INDEX   111

PREFACE

This book was originally issued in May 1969 as a RAND Corporation Research Memorandum prepared for the Department of Defense, Office of the Assistant Secretary of Defense (International Security Affairs). Except for some minor changes, the study appears as it was first issued. Essentially a *tour d'horizon,* it offers one approach to assessing the implications of the prospective security environment over roughly the next decade in Southeast Asia for United States policies. Certain policy changes are suggested in accordance with a definition of American national interests in Southeast Asia and conclusions about the nature and limitations of American responsibilities and influence in that region.

This study may be regarded as a point of departure for more detailed analyses. It assumes that if we are to reach decisions on the allocation of funds, arms, manpower, and commitments for coming years, we first need to examine American priorities and capabilities in a region that will likely remain politically and economically unstable for some time. The book presents one view of what those priorities should be and, in so doing, takes issue with several prevalent notions about Southeast Asia: that the outcome in Vietnam will critically affect regional security and the future of "wars of national liberation"; that the United

States, or the noncommunist nations of Asia independent of the United States, should be primarily interested in, and are capable of establishing, a balance of power against Communist China; and that the continual armed conflicts within individual countries are usually manufactured externally and in large part involve struggles between competing ideologies. With these and related opinions in mind, certain changes in American perceptions of Southeast Asia are proposed that may foster a different view of, and different policies to deal with, instability there. Concomitantly, recommendations are forwarded which, if implemented, might set in motion developments leading to opportunities for reduced tension, especially in Sino-American relations.

In preparing this study, I profited immensely from numerous comments by RAND colleagues and am especially grateful to Charles Cooper, Alice Langley Hsieh, William Jones, Konrad Kellen, Paul Langer, Colonel William E. Simons, William A. Stewart, and C. A. H. Thomson, all of whom offered extensive comments at various stages of the manuscript.

In the early stages of the writing, I worked in conjunction with Daniel I. Okimoto, a consultant to The RAND Corporation presently at Tokyo University. Many of his thoughtful contributions have been retained in the present version, and I am pleased to record here my indebtedness for them. Any errors or oversights are, of course, my responsibility.

M. G.

Santa Monica, California

SOUTHEAST ASIA
TOMORROW

I

INTRODUCTION:
THE STRATEGIC ASSESSMENT OF
SOUTHEAST ASIA IN
1954 AND ITS IMPLICATIONS

The strategic and political problems likely to confront the United States in Southeast Asia once the Vietnam conflict is resolved show a number of parallels to the Vietnam crisis of 1954 and its aftermath. Decision-makers at that time pondered the place of Vietnam within the overall security situation of Southeast Asia. In search of new concepts for regional defense, they tried to assess the magnitude and nature of the Sino-Soviet threat and the capacities of Southeast Asian nations to contribute to possible new security arrangements. American national interests in Southeast Asia underwent intensive scrutiny in anticipation of a major shift in the balance of power there. While the present Vietnam war continues, the United States will again be re-examining the overall shape of Southeast Asia's security and its role in that security. In this connection, a look back to 1954 may be useful.

During the first sixteen months of the Eisenhower Administration, US government thinking accepted the major premise articulated under Truman that Communist subversion, unless checked in Indochina, would inexorably undermine the rest of free Asia.[1] Apparently, all key ad-

[1] For background and documentation, see Melvin Gurtov, *The First Vietnam Crisis: Chinese Communist Strategy and United States Involvement, 1953–1954* (New York: Columbia University Press, 1967).

1

ministration spokesmen adhered to this "domino principle." Whether every nation in Asia was as uniformly vulnerable to communism as the domino principle implied was one of several critical questions apparently not seriously debated at any point during American involvement in Indochina's affairs prior to the Geneva Conference.

In May 1954, however, when the Geneva Conference began, the administration publicly modified its views. It no longer felt that the alternatives in the region were either military victory or regional defeat; it came instead to believe that the fall of Indochina, or perhaps of Vietnam alone, would not automatically entail the loss of all Southeast Asia. This profound shift in emphasis, which seemed to undercut the chief assumptions behind American involvement in Indochina, in part grew out of the consideration that the security of post-settlement Southeast Asia could be ensured even in the worst contingency—i.e., Communist governments in all three Indochinese states— through the formation of a regional system of defense (later the Southeast Asia Treaty Organization, SEATO).

What is significant for present events is the rationale which led the administration to believe that an effective SEATO could be formed. One reason relates to what might be called a regionalist conception of Southeast Asian problems. Eisenhower's Administration, like Truman's, regarded Southeast Asia as consisting of politically and culturally diverse nations whose only common denominators were anti-colonialism (in the sense that they rejected foreign control), geographical proximity, and a lack of anxiety about the Communist threat. While recognizing the heterogeneity of the nations there, however, the Eisenhower Administration paradoxically persisted in the belief that they could be welded together into a militarily useful anti-Communist front.

The disposition toward dealing with Southeast Asia in these incongruous terms stemmed also from the events of the day. At home, the government had to contend with Senator Joseph McCarthy's anti-Communist crusade. Abroad, following the armistice in Korea, threats of "massive retaliation" had not kept Communist China from providing material assistance to the Viet Minh. Communist guerrilla warfare was still active in Malaya. Moreover, the administration confronted what it believed to be a Soviet threat to Western Europe which had abated only marginally since Stalin's death. Faced with a wide range of real and potential dangers, and convinced that the monolithic Soviet bloc, represented in Asia by Peking, was engaging in a region-wide rather than country-by-country probe of Free World defenses, the administration found the regional approach to be the most logical path to security in the Pacific.

From the outset, the real difficulty of SEATO was not that certain Asian states were unconvinced of the need for American protection. What restricted SEATO's effectiveness was that the Asian governments made no commitment to come to one another's defense, never demonstrated willingness to come forward with the needed manpower, and, most important, some of them (as the April 1955 Afro-Asian conference in Bandung revealed) were giving serious consideration to alternative paths to security, such as nonalignment, that were free of the constraints of active association with either of the two major blocs. In short, while the United States tried in the post-Indochina environment to reduce its commitments to involvement in marginal conflicts while increasing the responsibilities of the Asian states, most of the Asian states preferred either to avoid involvement in a formal pact or to have American protection available without committing themselves to any substantive steps in advance.

What do the circumstances and strategic thinking of 1954 mean for American security planning now? The first lesson, now generally recognized, is that Southeast Asia cannot be treated as a solid bloc of uniformly motivated states. The very use of the term "Southeast Asia" creates the danger of formulating region-wide policies that fail to take account of significant political, social, and economic distinctions among and within nations of the region. The domino principle was geared precisely to the assumption that these nations were more or less equally open to penetration and subversion by international communism—that, in other words, their differences were largely irrelevant in the face of the omnipresent Communist threat. The continuing trend toward differentiation among Southeast Asian political systems calls for some important qualifications of the domino analogy. That trend may also have significance for proposals which would count heavily on American leadership in regional defense planning.

A second and related point stemming from the experiences of 1954 is the nature of the threat to Southeast Asia. SEATO was basically designed as the linchpin of a denial strategy: if the Soviets and Chinese were, as suspected, bent upon directly taking over or influencing the formation of neutral governments throughout Southeast Asia—both developments being regarded in Washington as inimical to US security interests—they would have to confront a united will based on Western-Asian cooperation. It is pertinent to gauge carefully the extent to which a united will exists today, as well as the nature of Soviet and Chinese ambitions in light of the Sino-Soviet rift, diversity in the international Communist movement, differences in the goals of the various Communist governments and parties in the region, and the implications of China's Cultural Revolution. An appraisal of the advantages and disadvantages of a containment strategy[2] and the dimensions of

---

[2] For one such appraisal, see David P. Mozingo, "Containment in Asia Reconsidered," *World Politics*, vol. XIX, no. 3 (April 1967), pp. 361–77.

the threat posed to our security interests also seems in order.

Third, the reaction to the 1954 crisis, so heavily weighted in favor of achieving regional security through the application of military power, failed to consider whether greater emphasis on economic and political stabilization and growth might not provide a more effective long-term answer to the threat of subversion. Regionalism as a military formula has turned out to have serious limitations, which perhaps can be overcome through less ambitious economic and social cooperative arrangements in which the American role is reduced. The persistent desire of the Southeast Asian nations for some assurance of durability in their relations with the major powers may not mean that they would unanimously accept American leadership or military alliances to achieve it.

Finally, there was in the mid-1950s a need for sharper conceptions of priorities in the national interest. Policy will tend to suffer so long as it is based, as in 1954, on spasmodic reactions to momentary pressures, fears, and senses of loss. Similarly, long-term planning without sufficient flexibility runs risks. In both cases, a constant process of clarifying US policy priorities can be useful if it focuses on the precise security interests which the United States must be committed to protect.

II

THE SECURITY PICTURE
IN SOUTHEAST ASIA

Regardless of the view one takes of the legitimacy and wisdom of the American involvement in Vietnam, a deep commitment of American prestige, manpower, money, and political credibility has occurred, and as a result every Asian nation has in some way been affected. How the war ends, consequently, is bound to have an important bearing on the shape of the future American role in Southeast Asia, even though a strong case might be made that one of the dominant reasons for the initial entry of the United States into Vietnam's struggle—to defeat an insurgency that would, if successful, be duplicated elsewhere in the under-developed world—was faulty. What needs to be assessed, then, is not the merits of America's involvement in Vietnam but its consequences for the security of Southeast Asia.

Vietnam: The Implications of Withdrawal

As negotiations between the United States and North Vietnam take their course in Paris, it is increasingly apparent that neither side can achieve complete military victory and compel the other to accept what would amount to a victor's peace. Ultimately, therefore, the critical questions will relate to the circumstances of the American withdrawal. In deciding upon withdrawal, the United States will probably want to ensure, first, that the Government of South Vietnam (GVN) retains the capability to be a contender against the Communist forces and, second, that the substance of any settlement becomes at least as much a Vietnamese as an American responsibility. Should the United States, after several years of intensive commitment, appear to have reduced the GVN's chances of survival to cut its own losses, or to have imposed a political and military settlement on the GVN, the Southeast Asian nations that have supported US policy would probably seriously reassess the advisability of close association with the United States.

Even if the United States can withdraw from South Vietnam under relatively favorable circumstances, and even if the withdrawal proceeds smoothly—i.e., the forces and bases are evacuated without interference; the South Vietnamese armed forces do not quickly collapse; and the Viet Cong, if included in a coalition government, find it in their interests to move cautiously while seeking to control the government—America's allies will still be seriously concerned. Having taken place under circumstances which imply that the United States will accept a GVN defeat, the withdrawal may have important political consequences for the particular governments committed to the support of American objectives (e.g., the Philippines). The argument here is not that such consequences can be avoided but that the United States may be able to reduce or offset them.

In the first place, official clarifications of American aims in Asia after withdrawal could greatly influence the extent of allied disturbance. Donald S. Zagoria's point in this regard seems especially relevant: "Most non-Communist Asian leaders do not fear an accommodation in Vietnam that could eventually bring Communists to power there so

8

much as they fear that from the one extreme of total involvement we will then shift to complete withdrawal from
the area."[1] The immediate reaction of several key Asian
leaders to President Johnson's March 31, 1968, speech
announcing a partial cessation of the bombing and his decision not to seek a second term in office bears out this
point. The leaders speculated that the United States might
not merely be contemplating withdrawal from Vietnam but
might also be laying the groundwork for a fortress-America
position in the succeeding Administration.

The anxieties of friendly Asian governments that a
phased withdrawal from Vietnam will be the prelude to
a total withdrawal from Asia can be alleviated by both
private and public communications and by appropriate
signals from leading administration spokesmen. After
Vietnam, most if not all of those governments will no
doubt still have a strong interest in maintaining close ties
to the United States, provided the United States indicates
that the interest is mutual. What may very well change
after withdrawal is the character of US relations with them.

American pronouncements that withdrawal will not upset the so-called balance of power in Asia will nevertheless
constitute an admission that the United States, as in 1954,
miscalculated the importance of Vietnam to the region's
security. But this admission can cut two ways: on one
side, certain allies will require more than verbal assurances
of a continuing American commitment to their defense if
they are not to alter their policies in ways undesirable to
the United States; on the other, the confidence of some
Asian (and non-Asian) governments in the wisdom and
restraint of America as a great power will be restored.
Official statements can be made that (a) stress the limited
damage of the Vietnam outcome, (b) point out that the

---

[1] "Who's Afraid of the Domino Theory?" *New York Times
Magazine* (April 21, 1968), p. 61.

United States has honorably and effectively fulfilled its commitment,[2] (c) conclude that South Vietnam's future rests (as American policy has always sought to ensure) in the hands of South Vietnamese, and (d) reaffirm the nation's intention to continue as an active partner in bringing about security and stability in Asia. Such statements will hardly be sufficient to end doubts, but they may reassure friendly nations during the critical period after withdrawal.

Verbal reassurances, insofar as they are directed to America's allies, will need to be backed by more tangible expressions of a continuing American commitment. Any immediate American shift in strategic orientation following withdrawal from Vietnam would seem to risk encouraging the very suspicions and abetting the very political instabilities that would jeopardize the implementation of new policies. Hence, it may be required that, in the interim after withdrawal (whether with or without a settlement), certain allied demands (e.g., from Thailand and South Korea) for additional economic and military support will have to be met.[3]

[2] It could also be made clear that American assistance to the GVN will continue or, in the event that withdrawal comes in the aftermath of a settlement, that the United States is prepared to assist any legally constituted, genuinely neutral Saigon government, whatever its political composition.

[3] Even in the event of a highly favorable end to the war—e.g., one that resulted in a gradual disintegration of the Viet Cong and the reduction of hostile action to sporadic incidents—allied demands would still be high. North Vietnam, having failed in the South, could at low cost step up assistance to the Pathet Lao, thereby imperiling Thai security along the Mekong and eliciting new Thai aid demands. The South Koreans, having assisted the American effort in Vietnam, could call for substantial reimbursement in military aid and a renewed American commitment to stand beside Seoul in the event of another outbreak of hostile action by the North Koreans. In a sense, then, closer American ties to allies will be dependent less on the kind of settlement achieved in Vietnam than on the decision of 1965 to broaden the base of allied support for the war.

10

Furthermore, the United States may be called upon to contribute more to the defense of Japan, the Philippines, and Nationalist China—support that will have political significance for the ruling parties in those countries no less than in South Korea and Thailand. Finally, certain allies (Australia and New Zealand) and certain noncontributing friendly nations (Malaysia, Singapore, and perhaps Indonesia), although not directly affected by a withdrawal from Vietnam, may be expected to voice anxieties about future Communist intentions in the region, to take a fresh look at their security requirements, and to sound out American (and British) leaders on their defense plans for the region. In fact, those five nations met at Kuala Lumpur in the spring of 1968 to consider the prospects for defense cooperation in their subregion.[4]

In all these matters, the choice before the United States will be critical in many ways: the allocation of aid will have to be decided in the light of the predictably adverse domestic reaction in the United States to further commitments in Asia; any American assistance will run the risk of being interpreted, at home or abroad, as a serious commitment; Asian nations may form new alliances which will tend to cut across present American obligations under multilateral and bilateral treaties and may compel a re-

[4] There are likely to be varying kinds of "agonizing reappraisals" in the Indonesia Oceania area. The recent remarks of Professor Hedley Bull, the influential strategic analyst of the Australian National University, illustrate this point. In a speech entitled "The Political and Strategic Background to Australian Defense," Bull argued in favor of limited ("aloof") Australian cooperation with Malaysia, Singapore, and Indonesia, closer defense ties to New Zealand, and various measures to create a larger American stake in Australian security. His assumptions were "that new commitments entered into by the United States are extremely improbable, that a scaling down of existing commitments is very likely, and that a drastic reorientation of American policy in the area cannot be altogether excluded." (Speech before the Economic Society of Australia and New Zealand, 10th Autumn Forum [Victoria], May 1968.)

assessment of the latter. How the United States will re-spond to these early demands and expectations of friendly Asian nations is therefore likely to have relevance for US policy over the next decade. The distinctions that will have to be made between stop-gap assistance and long-term commitments will depend on more fundamental issues: the nature of the security threat in Southeast Asia; the inter-pretation of American interests in Asia (see chapter 3); and projected security-related developments in the region over the coming decade (see chapter 4).

The Meaning of Vietnam for Southeast Asia's Security

The kind of response the United States makes to its friends in Southeast Asia will largely be determined by the way Washington views Vietnam's significance for South-east Asia. In the short term, certain declaratory positions may have to be adopted and certain tangible compensa-tions made in order that a less-than-satisfactory outcome in Vietnam will not result in a drastic decline in Asian confidence in the United States. Over the longer run, how-ever, conditions in Southeast Asia are such that revolu-tionary movements of varying dimensions and composition may well reappear. When they do, there is the danger that declaratory policies will be treated as mere tactical devices and not as evidence of a serious reappraisal of the Vietnam experience. The critical question of whether and how the United States is prepared to respond in the future to Com-munist-supported subversion will remain unanswered.

In the intense debate over the broad significance of the Vietnam conflict, widely divergent positions have been adopted. On one side, it is asserted that a Communist Vietnam would pave the way, over time, for the political if not the military domination of Southeast Asia by pro-Communist forces. Should the Peking-Hanoi alliance succeed in Vietnam, it is argued, other insurgent movements will be encouraged to follow suit. Ranged on the other side are those who propose that Vietnam is such a unique experience that a Communist success there, far from predetermining the political orientation of other nations, might actually signal the last gasp of Asian communism. An independent Vietnam state, even under Communist control, cannot significantly influence insurgency elsewhere; to the contrary, all insurgencies are essentially determined by local circumstances. As is frequently the case, room can be found between these two sharply contrasting hypotheses.

The position taken in this study is that while Vietnam does seem to be an atypical case, and while the domino theory seems to exaggerate grossly the extent of the Communist threat to Southeast Asia under the impact of a Viet Cong success, there are strong grounds for believing that an all-Communist Vietnam would pose a substantial threat to Indochina's stability. North Vietnam's intentions are considered to be distinct from those of Communist China; but Peking may, under certain conditions, continue to encourage liberation movements regardless of the outcome in Vietnam. The meaning of Vietnam is therefore dealt with, first, in terms of the domino thesis and its relationship to North Vietnamese ambitions, and, second, in terms of Communist China's probable reactions to a Vietnam situation which, because of an American withdrawal, will appear potentially favorable to the Vietnamese Communists.

The Domino Effect and North Vietnam. The war in Vietnam has been the product of circumstances which are not typical of those found elsewhere in Southeast Asia. Vietnam was a colony for nearly seventy-five years and finally gained independence as a divided state with a proviso for eventual unification. Nationalism has been a politically dynamic force there since early in the twentieth century. During the period of the first Indochina war, the Viet Minh were widely considered the best-organized vehicle for expressing political opposition; the Communist party captured nationalistic sentiment by displaying its potential to succeed militarily and by demonstrating effective, indeed charismatic, leadership; and, finally, non-Communist nationalists never demonstrated the organizational ability and leadership nor commanded the popular support needed to compete effectively with the Communists. In 1965, when the US military forces began to play a major role in the Vietnam conflict, the southern government was still seeking a genuine national leader while the National Liberation Front (NLF) had already woven itself into the political fabric of the South. By that time, too, the Communist military organization—the Viet Cong—had achieved a strength and sophistication that made it a formidable enemy.

It is possible to conclude from these circumstances that, especially with the end of the colonial era during which the Vietnamese Communist movement first thrived, other Communist-inspired and/or Communist-supported revolutionary movements will for the most part grow or wither, succeed or fail, independent of the outcome in Vietnam.[5] Nevertheless, certain pro-Communist revolutionary movements do not, and cannot, exist without outside logistical support, and where the capability exists for outside forces not only to stimulate by example but also to assist directly, the atypical features of the Vietnam experience may not entirely neutralize the danger of continuing insurgencies.

Consequently, the so-called stimulation effect of a less-

---

[5] This point has been made in different ways by Herbert S. Dinerstein, *Intervention against Communism* (Baltimore: The Johns Hopkins Press, 1967); and Paul Kecskemeti, *Insurgency as a Strategic Problem* (Santa Monica, Calif.: The RAND Corporation, Research Memorandum RM-5160-PR, February 1967).

than-satisfactory Vietnam outcome may be meaningful, but only where at least three additional elements are present: the ability of an insurgent organization to draw upon the material resources of an outside power; the ability of an insurgent force to create a sound politico-military organization; and the insurgent's ability to capitalize on deep-seated popular grievances and to use resources effectively.

There is a historical precedent for these conclusions. Consideration of the different impacts that the Chinese Communists' victory in 1949 had on revolutions then in progress in Burma and Vietnam appears to indicate that the stimulation effect is unlikely to prove decisive if confined to psychological encouragement. In the case of Burma, by 1950 the Communist Red and White Flags were at the peak of their offensive against government forces, and when the Chinese Communists took full control of the mainland, the Communist Party of Burma (CPB) evidently expected to receive equipment and supplies from them. But it did not. Similar expectations held in the Viet Minh camp were met when the Chinese People's Republic (CPR) began regular shipments of supplies across the border and accepted Viet Minh soldiers for political and military training. Leaving aside the reasons for the CPR's reluctance to do the same for the Burmese Communists, the point is that without material aid from China, they could not translate the uplifting news of a Communist success in China into a real capacity to sustain their revolutionary struggle. More important, even with Chinese assistance the Burmese Communists may still have lacked the crucial ingredient for success—the kind of tight-knit, disciplined organization present in Vietnam for exploiting widespread discontent among the peasantry and intellectuals. Then, as today, the Burmese Communists were severely hampered by personal factionalism which made for uncertain leadership in both party and military affairs. And in Burma, of course, the ruling government could claim the credit for having achieved independence. Analogies are always imperfect, but the Burma case does seem to support the view that a Viet Cong victory is unlikely of itself to guarantee success for other revolutionaries, any more than a Viet Cong defeat would augur failure.[6]

On the other hand, control of South Vietnam by the NLF would have important consequences for the security of Laos, Cambodia, and perhaps Thailand. The history of Vietnamese Communist activities in the Indochina region suggests that the Hanoi regime may not be content with accomplishing its major objective of national unification. As a Comintern agent, Ho Chi Minh was an active political organizer in northeast Thailand during the late 1920s.[7] The first Vietnamese Communist organization, it will be recalled, was the Indochinese Communist Party (ICP) headed by Ho, who by 1931 was also chief coordinator of the Comintern's Southeast Asia Bureau. Later, even though the ICP was said to have been dissolved, the Vietnamese Communists became the prime backers of the nascent resistance movements in Laos and Cambodia in the early 1950s. At the 1954 Geneva Conference, the Viet Minh spoke on behalf of these offshoot organizations, which were not represented. Since then, of course, North Vietnamese supplies and cadres have been the backbone

[6] After all, the defeat of the Viet Cong—by which is presumably meant compelling them to surrender, to desert, or to "melt away" into the jungles—could be twisted easily by Communists elsewhere to mean that while the "imperialists" prevailed, the NLF proved how vulnerable the leading imperialist power is and how fundamentally correct is the doctrine of protracted struggle. Dedicated Communist revolutionaries also could easily conclude that the United States, even if successful in Vietnam, would be unlikely to make the same sacrifices soon again.

[7] See Bernard B. Fall, *The Two Viet-Nams: A Political and Military Analysis* (New York: Frederick A. Praeger, 1965), p. 94.

16

or the Pathet Lao;[8] since about 1951 Thai-Lao cadres have been trained in the Democratic Republic of Vietnam (DRV) for political activity in the northeast of Thailand; and the so-called Khmer Viet Minh have been accused by Cambodian leaders of fomenting dissidence (with Viet Cong assistance) in several provinces along Cambodia's western, northern, and eastern frontiers.[9] With large Vietnamese populations in northeast Thailand[10] and eastern Cambodia, and with a veteran insurgent organization in Laos, North Vietnam is in a position to rebuild the foundations for in Indochinese federation.

The extent of North Vietnamese ambitions in Laos, Cambodia, and Thailand remains unclear. Much will depend on developments in South Vietnam, the timetable of North-South unification, the pace of the DRV's recovery from the bombing, and the policies and actions of the United States. Thus, it is difficult to foretell whether, for example, the DRV will be interested in asserting Vietnamese influence over parts of Laos and Cambodia or in

[8] Personal testimony on this point by a defected North Vietnamese captain is now available in Paul F. Langer and Joseph J. Zasloff, *The North Vietnamese Military Adviser in Laos: A First Hand Account* (Santa Monica, Calif.: The RAND Corporation, Research Memorandum RM-5688-ARPA, July 1968).

[9] As one example, see the editorial "Les coups pleuvent sur le Cambodge" in the semi-official *Réalités cambodgiennes*, no. 608 (July 26, 1968), pp. 3–5. Prince Sihanouk has, in addition, spoken out on the Khmer Viet Minh—Viet Cong—Pathet Lao relationship many times since late 1967.

[10] The Vietnamese population in northeast Thailand, which once numbered roughly 70,000 (and may now number anywhere from 40,000 to 75,000), consists mainly of refugees who either fled the three Indochinese states over a period of about two decades before the end of World War II or emigrated to the northeast during the French Indochina War. Some were reportedly active during the Laos conflicts of the late 1950s and early 1960s; see George Modelski. "The Viet Minh Complex," in Cyril E. Black and Thomas P. Thornton (eds.), *Communism and Revolution: The Strategic Uses of Political Violence* (Princeton, N.J.: (Princeton University Press, 1964), pp. 199–200.

attempting to bring about the installation of neighboring governments friendly to Hanoi. What is clear is that the DRV will be in a strong position, upon the withdrawal of American forces from South Vietnam, to exploit its military superiority by exerting varying forms of pressure on neighboring countries at very low cost and risk.[11]

A combination of positive American statements and actions on one side, and continuing uncertainty among Asian governments on the other, may actually strengthen regional security as a whole. If, for example, Southeast Asian nations begin thinking about forming an effective regional military alliance to combat Communist insurgencies (South Korea and Malaysia separately broached the idea publicly in early 1968), or if the American withdrawal gives impetus to more serious discussion of regional economic cooperation (a concept the Thai government is stressing), then potentially adverse developments in Vietnam may in the long term be turned to advantage elsewhere. Perceiving a Communist threat, yet uncertain about the American commitment, some Southeast Asian nations may be disposed to lean less heavily on American guidance and support. Events in Vietnam may prompt them to deal more decisively than in the past with the kinds of problems that Communist movements exploit. Should this reaction set in, the long-standing American aim of seeing the governments of the region contribute the

---

[11] It might be contended that after the war North Vietnam will be too preoccupied with reconstruction at home and implementation of a political settlement in the South to be of much assistance to the Pathet Lao. This argument might go on to posit that assurance of a favorable outcome in the South would obviate the DRV's need for the Ho Chi Minh route through Laos and Cambodia. These points may well be valid, but they seem to ignore the fact that most of the Pathet Lao units are situated outside the Ho Trail regions and that the Khmer Viet Minh have been active in central and western Cambodia no less than in the provinces bordering Vietnam.

18

predominant share toward their own stability will have been greatly furthered.

Southeast Asian politics are thus sufficiently diverse to make tenuous any assumptions about policy gains and losses. Any Vietnam outcome is bound to have important positive as well as negative effects and, in the case of the latter, these frequently will be susceptible to reversal or reduction.

China and Insurgency. In addition to contrasting views on the implications of a Viet Cong success for revolutionary warfare in the underdeveloped world, there are also basic differences among Asian analysts over Communist China's commitment to a people's war. One view is that Communist China will be encouraged by a Vietnam outcome favorable to Communist forces to sustain its assault on non-Communist nations in Asia toward the end of subordinating lesser powers to political and economic dependencies of Peking. Others contend that while Peking may be pleased with a Communist victory in Vietnam, the Chinese are so involved in internal problems and so aware of the numerous limitations on their power in Southeast Asia that they will remain as reluctant as before to go beyond bellicose pronouncements. Again, it seems advisable to strike a medium between these divergent positions.

Although an American withdrawal from Vietnam would dovetail with Chinese regional objectives, the fact that Peking consistently opposed DRV-US negotiations will deflate Chinese claims to omniscience in dealing with "the imperialists." Furthermore, in gaining, or in seeming to have influenced, the removal of American forces and bases from South Vietnam, the DRV will have demonstrated anew its ability to deal effectively with the "imperialist camp" without having to rely on guidance from Peking. Hanoi's consistent claim to military and political creativity

19

in applying Marxism-Leninism to the special conditions of Vietnam will have been proved "correct"—a considerable ideological victory.

On balance, however, the Chinese will have achieved their primary objective of eliminating a major American "position of strength" in Southeast Asia. Even though the particular Vietnamese national liberation movement led by the Lao Dong and the NLF will have been successful because they adroitly reformulated, and on occasion rejected, Maoist military tenets, the CPR may still proclaim the outcome a major triumph for Chinese-style people's war, one worthy of emulation by other revolutionary movements engaged in armed struggle against "reactionary" regimes.

The crucial issue, however, is whether the Chinese, in the flush of a settlement advantageous to DRV interests, will be stimulated to increase assistance to other areas, that have a potential for people's war. In the course of the Cultural Revolution, the Peking news media have stressed that rebel groups in Thailand, Indonesia, Malaysia, India, Burma, the Philippines, and Laos can profit from Mao's theories and the Vietnamese Communists' experience. It would hardly be surprising, then, if in the aftermath of a Viet Cong success Chinese propaganda efforts were intensified. The United States may have convinced China (as was apparently the case in 1965) of its preparedness to resist Communist-backed revolutionary war, but Vietnam may have confirmed Mao in his belief that a well-organized capably led people's war conducted in accordance with his theories can, with small but critical outside support, inflict heavy damage on better-armed enemies and increase the effect of "contradictions" in the "imperialist camp."[12]

---

[12] Paul Kecskemeti has made a complementary point. He observes that inasmuch as the United States intervened in Vietnam to restore the *status quo ante*, an American success would not "prove" that aggression does not pay. "[T]he precedent of a defensive success need not deter further aggressive probing. Whenever it appears doubtful that the United States will intervene, or

Should the Viet Cong in fact surmount the obstacles posed by the American presence and gain their objectives through negotiations or otherwise, insurgent organizations in Southeast Asia may become increasingly receptive to Chinese liberation warfare propaganda; but this potentiality—to reiterate an earlier point—will not necessarily guarantee the rise of a significant insurgent threat.

Actually, the extent to which the CPR will be able to exploit revolutionary situations such as Vietnam will probably be limited by at least three factors. In the first place, the Chinese apparently remain aware that an insurgent success in one area may in the short run encourage other movements to become tactically more audacious and more conscious of the need to develop broad popular backing and solid military and political organizations (the traditional "tripod" of army, party, and united front). They seem equally aware that such movements ultimately cannot succeed on the sole basis of outside stimulation and support. As Lin Piao stipulated in his famous article of September 3, 1965, national liberation movements must practice "self-reliance," for outside assistance can be significant only in proportion to the internal capacity of an insurgent movement for sustained growth.[13]

---

that it has enough time to intervene with effect before a *fait accompli* is secured, Communist powers can afford to experiment with local probing moves, In view of the fact that their existing holdings are secure." The deterrent effect of a Vietnam victory would therefore "be conditional and incomplete. It would only extend to those cases in which successful intervention would be credible on grounds of feasibility, cost, and risk." Future Vietnams would, by this logic, be very attractive to the Communists; but as Kecskemeti goes on to comment, insurgencies of the Vietnam type, in which the Communists appear as the saviors of nationalism, are very unlikely to recur. See Kecskemeti, *Insurgency as a Strategic Problem*, p. 11.

[13] See the analysis by David P. Mozingo and Thomas W. Robinson, *Lin Piao on "People's War": China Takes a Second Look at Vietnam* (Santa Monica, Calif.: The RAND Corporation, Research Memorandum RM-4814-PR, November 1965).

21

Even where the capacity for self-reliance exists, Lin strongly implied, China will be guided in its choice of revolutionary allies by Chinese interests, in particular by the nature of the regime against which violent action is contemplated. Thus, depending largely upon the attitude a non-Communist government adopts toward China, and especially the character of its affiliations with the United States and the Soviet Union, Peking may provide some mixture of political and (indirect) military support to the anti-government forces or may (as in pre-Cultural Revolution policies toward Burma and Cambodia) seek to further Chinese interests by ignoring the existing or potential insurrectionary strength in favor of "people's diplomacy."[14]

Second, Peking seems to have undertaken a reassess-

---

[14] As David P. Mozingo has commented: "Peking's actual behavior and her ideological theses on revolution reveal that she is prepared to refrain from direct interference in the competition (whether peaceful or violent) between Communist parties and the 'bourgeois' classes in Asian countries, so long as the United States also does not directly intervene in these countries' politics. . . . China argues that the Communist bloc should try to deter, or by various means oppose, attempts by the United States to use her own power unilaterally to determine the outcome of the competition between the bourgeois elites and the Communist forces. The Chinese leaders' view of their own national interests requires this position, for they regard the United States as bent on organizing all Asia into a belt of client-states opposing Peking. . . . China's call to 'revolution' [hence] is directed primarily to existing and potential elites in Asia and elsewhere whom she regards as likely to share with her an interest in altering any status quo imposed by U.S. or Soviet policies." (Mozingo, "Containment in Asia," pp. 368–69.)

Mozingo's argument might be considered dated with the apparent upsurge of Chinese militancy during the Cultural Revolution. I will contend, however, that the Cultural Revolution should be understood as a peculiar phenomenon of domestic Chinese politics. For a brief interlude in 1967, the Revolution did have a critical impact on China's foreign relations in that it encouraged ultraleftist elements in some CPR embassies and offices abroad to propagandize Maoism. But Chinese foreign policy does not seem to have changed then or since, and foreign relations have gradually returned to "normalcy." See note following.

ment in the fall of 1967 of the costs and benefits of exporting the Cultural Revolution. Prior to about September 1967, Mao's evident determination to revolutionize Chinese society had been projected abroad,[15] especially after the work of professionals in the foreign ministry came under attack and close scrutiny by "revolutionary rebels." With the relatively more conservative approach to foreign policy-making temporarily unrepresented, and with numerous Chinese ambassadors and their staffs recalled to Peking, the way was apparently cleared for the dissemination of revolutionary materials by the New China News Agency and by skeleton embassy staffs in foreign capitals. It quickly became apparent, however, not only in Burma, Cambodia, Nepal, and Ceylon but also in several African and West European countries, that such efforts to export Maoism would not be tolerated. Peking had violated its own principle of noninterference in the internal affairs of friendly nations and had been rebuffed.

The steady erosion of China's reputation resulting from these events, coupled with the onset of grave administrative problems within China, apparently persuaded Mao and Lin to move gradually toward a restoration of friendly ties to Ceylon, Cambodia, and Nepal, and domestically toward recapturing the loyalty of cadres deemed vital to effective administration at all levels of government. China's attitude did not change toward some of its other neighbors (notably, Burma), but the events of 1967 may have demonstrated anew to Peking the limits other governments place on friendly relations with China. In fact, the residue of suspicion which Chinese activities undoubtedly left throughout Southeast Asia will probably be a strong im-

[15] For more detailed comments on the relationship of domestic to foreign policy during the Cultural Revolution phase, see Melvin Gurtov, *The Foreign Ministry and Foreign Affairs in China's "Cultural Revolution"* (Santa Monica, Calif.: The RAND Corporation, Research Memorandum RM-5934-PR, March 1969).

petus for all governments to guard against foreign and local Communist agitation.

A final, and perhaps the most significant, point is that in the event of China's active, although indirect, support of certain attractive revolutionary situations, the capability, effectiveness, and environment of insurgent forces may be beyond decisive Chinese influence. China's training of cadres, tactical advice, and logistical support may be forthcoming, but it cannot ensure that the insurgents will have the organizational acumen, leadership, popular support, or military skills to overcome their opposition. Nor can the various forms of Chinese assistance create the anti-colonialist nationalism which seems to have been so central to the Vietnamese Communist movement's appeal. The contingency of Chinese aid, in short, needs to be considered within the framework of vastly different security environments once the United States withdraws from Vietnam.

All of this, of course, is not to argue that China will absolutely refrain from assisting certain revolutions in Southeast Asia. China's sense of priorities would seem to call for low-risk support of those anti-reactionary, anti-imperialist movements which hold out the potential for directly or indirectly hastening the removal of American and "revisionist" (Soviet) influence from China's periphery. This major Chinese objective—to eliminate or paralyze antagonistic sources of competitive power and influence in areas deemed to fall within China's "sphere of influence"—and the limitations of geography make it likely that, after Vietnam, Peking's principal nondiplomatic interests in Southeast Asia will be Thailand, Laos, and Burma.

A US withdrawal from Vietnam followed by the gradual removal of American airmen and strategic aircraft from Thai bases—a not unlikely development in view of recent Thai statements—might reduce Chinese anxieties and shift the consequent pressures considerably. The CPR, beginning in the fall of 1964, publicly offered its support to the weak Communist Party of Thailand (CPT) and subsequently to the party's front organizations. The primary motivation for those moves seems to have been to warn the Thai government of China's capability to make life difficult for Bangkok in the north and northeast in the event the Royal Thai Government (RTG) sustained its support of the American effort in Vietnam and Laos, and implemented plans to provide facilities for use by the US Air Force against targets in North Vietnam. In the wake of a Vietnam withdrawal, then, the extent of Chinese support of the CPT-sponsored rebellion could depend on the nature of the Thai-American alliance. Should Bangkok demonstrate its self-reliance by requesting a sharp reduction in the number of US military personnel in the country, back to the pre-1965 level, the Chinese might see advantages to practicing greater restraint, even if Thailand retained formal defense ties with the United States through SEATO.[16] Peking's restraint could take the form of a reduction or elimination of Thai-language broadcasts, which provide the CPT and its fronts with a political platform, or a decrease in the limited flow of arms to the rebels.

Barring such a change in Thai policy, China will probably continue its low-cost collaboration with the DRV in support of the Pathet Lao as well as the CPT. Conceivably, though, the Chinese may not see their interests served by an expansion of North Vietnam's territory or

[16] George Modelski makes the important observation that Peking's concern over developments in Thailand during the last several years has revolved not about Bangkok's links to SEATO but about the presence of foreign (i.e., US) military personnel on Thai soil seemingly threatening Laos, such as the 5,000 US troops stationed in Thailand during the 1962 Laotian crisis. See his "Thailand and China: From Avoidance to Hostility," in A. M. Halpern (ed.), *Policies toward China: Views from Six Continents* (New York: McGraw-Hill Book Company, 1965), p. 361.

25

political influence in Indochina. A "Greater Vietnam" federation might be viewed from Peking as a challenge to Chinese claims to paramount influence in the Indochina region. Hanoi's domination of that region could pose difficulties for the CPR if aggressive behavior by the North Vietnamese prompted threats of retaliatory action or increased American assistance to the neutral and rightist Laotian factions.

Today, as in the past, China's primary goal is to free Thailand and Laos, like Cambodia, from US influence. The Chinese are surely aware that North Vietnam's pursuit of its own national and revolutionary objectives in Laos and northeast Thailand might lead to another round of American intervention in Laotian affairs. Although the prospects are slim, it is conceivable that the CPR would be amenable to a new international conference on Laos— either concurrent with, or after, the Vietnam negotiations —which would reinforce the guarantees pledged in 1962 and thereby lessen the prospects for a return of American power to the Asia mainland. Peking might also regard contributing to a reaffirmation of Laotian neutrality as a means of restoring China's tarnished image of standard-bearer of the five principles of peaceful coexistence. In any event, the Thai attitude may be crucial, for if Bangkok were to reduce the American presence in north and northeast Thailand, China might find added incentive to cut back open support of the Pathet Lao in the interest of achieving its broader objective of a nonhostile, neutralized belt of mainland Southeast Asian nations.

China's apparent reappraisal in late 1967 of the Cultural Revolution's impact on foreign policy did not extend to an immediate attempt to improve relations with Burma. Peking had already made a verbal commitment to the overthrow of the Ne Win regime by violent revolution and had attached labels to Ne Win (e.g., "Burma's Chiang Kai-shek," "lackey of the revisionists and the imperialists") which could not easily be retracted. The Burmese

White Flag Communists had already been encouraged and given some material support to intensify their revolution. Events of the summer of 1967, moreover, had led to serious government-approved anti-Chinese rioting, a number of deaths, and the imprisonment of some low-ranking CPR nationals, making it difficult for any Chinese government to accept a restoration of the *status quo ante* without seeming to have suffered a humiliating rebuff from the Rangoon government. These and other factors set the Burma case apart from events in Nepal, Ceylon, and Cambodia, where propaganda activities sponsored by the Chinese embassies did not get out of hand. Finally, the Ne Win government had, since late 1966 (dating from the General's visit to the United States), moved gradually away from a sheltered isolationism and toward more open contact with the Soviet Union and the United States. Amid the then intense atmosphere in Peking, these moves may have been mistakenly interpreted as signs of a Burmese departure from neutralism.

The extent of direct Chinese assistance to the White Flags and those ethnic minority bands willing to work with the Communists is not clear. What is important is that China's ability to manipulate events in Burma seems quite limited. Typically, Peking has called for the CPB–White Flags to adhere closely to Mao's teachings on the necessity for building a strong party, disciplined army, and broad united front; and the White Flags have openly acknowledged the guiding role of Mao's "thoughts." But the White Flags suffer the malaise of factionalism common to all the rebellious groups in Burma, and there is no evidence to demonstrate that the party is any more successful now at adapting Maoism to Burmese conditions than previously.[17] In addition, Peking's support cannot overcome the

[17] To the contrary, since early 1967 the White Flags under Thakin Than Tun have had to weather a number of reported purges of "revisionist" elements that would seem to have reduced the leadership's numbers dramatically. Than Tun himself was slain by a one-time follower in 1968.

problems of terrain which reduce Communist coordination, the dissimilarities of both ideological viewpoint and objectives among the Communist and ethnic rebels, and the general peasant support of the government. These factors combine to make the White Flags uncertain allies of Peking, as was no doubt the case in 1950. As long as the revolutionary government does not use the occasion of deteriorating relations to move too far toward either the United States or the USSR—and Ne Win has been careful to do neither—the chance remains good that Sino-Burmese relations may gradually revert to their former state of détente based on the principle of mutual noninterference.[18]

The extent of China's interest in returning to a working relationship with Burma could depend on the state of Sino-Indian relations. As in 1960, when the CPR was evidently motivated to reach a border accord with Rangoon partly in order to further isolate New Delhi, China may again seek to play off one neighbor against another. Most recently, however, when China's relations with both India and Burma have been strained, the Chinese provided training and propaganda materials to members of certain factions of the Naga and Mizo autonomous movements which have long been operating in the Assam border region. Yet this support may be seen less as a direct Chinese commitment to the success of the Nagas and Mizos than as the conclusion of a temporary, tactical alliance with yet another force working against established governments not

[18] There were already signs in 1968 of improvement in Sino-Burmese relations: a noticeable softening of China's propaganda attacks on Ne Win; the attendance of Chinese officials at important official ceremonies in Rangoon; and the participation of Burmese officials in Chinese embassy functions. An important future indicator of China's attitude will be the fate of the Sino-Burmese Treaty of Friendship and Mutual Non-Aggression (January 28, 1960), which will not expire in 1971 unless one of the parties gives advance notice of a desire to terminate the treaty.

to Peking's liking. China's backing of the Nagas and Mizos, as of other minority tribes, is still minuscule; its influence is likely to be determined mainly, if not entirely, by the rebels' cohesion and by the effectiveness and liberality of the Indian and Burmese governments in dealing with the tribes' demands. Should Sino-Burmese relations improve, Peking would doubtless be perfectly prepared to support the claims of only the Nagas in India and drop further attention to the same peoples living on the Burma side of the border.

Conclusion. A settlement in Vietnam favorable to the Communists would appear likely to produce a mixed bag of relatively advantageous and relatively disadvantageous developments in Southeast Asia. Neither extremely pessimistic expectations of region-wide Communist revolutionary outbursts nor extremely sanguine assumptions of the confinement of Vietnam's impact to Vietnam alone would seem adequate to convey the complexity of Southeast Asian politics and the motivations of the leading Communist powers there. A less-than-satisfactory outcome in South Vietnam cannot be readily isolated from the mainstream of Asian governmental opinion nor from the impetus it may give to North Vietnam to seek the attainment of its military and political objectives in Indochina. But such an outcome need not be regarded, either by the United States or by its allies, as the forerunner to other Vietnams, as a guarantee that other insurgencies will be encouraged, nor as a denial of common interests with long-time allies in a secure Southeast Asia.

The challenge to the United States will be to soften the impact of a withdrawal from Vietnam. Diplomatic efforts to dispel fears of an American pullout from Asia and a responsiveness to the material and political needs of allied nations should help to retard any momentum toward serious estrangement from United States policies and programs. It is also important to recognize that doubts about American intentions in Southeast Asia may, if kept within bounds, actually promote genuine self-reliance. If the United States reconsiders the relevance of Vietnam to China's regional objectives and undertakes a narrower assessment of the meaning of Vietnam, the essentially ambiguous results of the Vietnam experience may be better appreciated and an overreaction avoided. Improvement of the security situation in Southeast Asia in the aftermath of a Vietnam withdrawal would be promoted more readily through a mutual recognition and acceptance by the region's nations and by the United States of the limitations to their relationships than through an attempt to restore relations to their former apparent closeness.

III

AMERICAN INTERESTS IN SOUTHEAST ASIA

Approaches to Delineating the National Interest

The national interest of the United States, it is generally agreed, demands a certain measure of involvement in Asian affairs. The chief difficulty has always lain in drawing up criteria which can give the term "national interest" operational meaning.

One approach is to differentiate between the practical and ideological components of the national interest. An example is Ernest R. May's contention that American "policy" really seems to involve two different interests: the "calculated" ones, arising out of careful measurement of costs and benefits, capabilities, and enemy intentions, and the "axiomatic" policies, flowing from deeply held tenets of American tradition.[1] This distinction, however, may be more useful in examining past policies than in formulating new ones. The future objective situation is by nature open to varying interpretations. Moreover, changes in the traditional values of decision-makers occur slowly and involve the near-impossible task of identifying values and weighing their influence on decision-making. The problem in-

[1] Ernest R. May, "The Nature of Foreign Policy: The Calculated versus the Axiomatic," *Daedalus* (September 1962), pp. 653–67.

31

evitably arises that, depending upon the country under discussion, certain traditional values may outweigh the more calculated ones; precisely what mixture of the calculated and the axiomatic is appropriate frequently becomes a matter of time, circumstance, and sentiment.

A similar analytical problem arises if the national interest is broken down into substantive components of the "value" of Southeast Asian countries to the United States.[2] Each nation of the region has by itself little or no relevance to the defense and well-being of the United States; the hostile domination of any single nation could not directly threaten the physical or economic security of the United States. On the economic side, according to 1966 statistics, Southeast Asia accounted for only 7 percent of total US exports and accounted for 8 percent of total US imports.[3] Private long-term direct investments overseas by Americans (in 1964) were about $44.3 billion, of which only about $3.2 billion went into the countries of Asia and Oceania.[4] Yet certain countries in the region may have value to the United States for psychological, cultural, and historical reasons which defy numerical or logistical analysis.

A third approach to defining the national interest rests on the belief that the United States must maintain a classic balance of power around China's frontiers. This argument has recently been expounded by Fred Greene. He contends that the vital American interest is to "check"

[2] For a discussion of this approach and its limitations, see Charles Wolf, Jr., *Some Aspects of the "Value" of Less-Developed Countries to the United States* (Santa Monica, Calif.: The RAND Corporation, Paper P-2649, October 1962); and Charles Wolf, Jr., *United States Interests in Asia* (Santa Monica, Calif.: The RAND Corporation, Paper P-3311, January 1966), a statement before the Subcommittee on the Far East and the Pacific of the House Foreign Affairs Committee.

[3] U.S. Bureau of the Census, *Statistical Abstract of the United States: 1967*, Vol. 88, p. 840.

[4] *Ibid.*, p. 815.

Chinese power by assuring "the preservation of Japan, Pakistan, and India, as well as the strategically essential access states, the Philippines and Australia."[5] But the attachment of priorities to American interests and attempts to determine which developments inimical to US interests are more or less likely to occur, he later argues, are of little help in times of revolutionary change. Thus, containment of Chinese power within the "intermediate power zone" (i.e., among the smaller, less powerful states of the region) must also be accomplished because, despite the low priority of that area for US security, "an effective and timely response . . . may improve the American position throughout the region simply because it represents a successful demonstration of US power and will. These results might more than compensate for the 'inefficient' expenditures involved."[6]

The difficulties raised by these approaches to delineating the national interest need not mean that a clearer portrayal of it is beyond reach. While the US interest involves combinations of tangible and intangible factors (the military versus the psychological, the economic versus the political, and the calculated versus the axiomatic), the factors do seem describable in a way that permits discrimination between American relations with one country and another. Even then, of course, the American interest cannot be said to have been determined, for it often happens that interests (in the broadest sense) in one nation conflict with different, possibly higher (more vital) interests in another.[7] However, by analyzing American relations with

[5] *U.S. Policy and the Security of Asia* (New York: McGraw-Hill Book Company, 1968), p. 36; see also chapters III and IV.

[6] *Ibid.*, pp. 58–59.

[7] Three types of conflicting interests come to mind. In one sense, conflicts may arise between strictly American ideals, such as between the promotion of self-determination and the formation of democratic governments, or between political support for independent states and the achievement of a détente with a hostile

Southeast Asian nations in terms of critical elements, as opposed to desirable long-term goals, it may be possible to establish the baselines for policy recommendations. The denial of this "priorities" approach, explicit in Greene's analysis, is in essence an argument against change, based on the view that any change might upset the supposedly precarious power balance. Yet if certain Asian nations can be identified as particularly vital to American interests, some changes, perhaps involving a redistribution of military and political power and influence, might not only be possible but also better preserve those interests while promoting others.

Vital American Interests in Southeast Asia

American interests in Southeast Asia may become less abstruse if we list five critical (special and important) elements which comprise them. These elements are: (1) security—those changes of political systems which, by leading or threatening to lead to domination by a hostile power, would pose a danger to the immediate or potential

---

government. At another level, American interests may clash with the equally legitimate interests of other (friendly) governments. For instance, the presumed American desire to bolster the stability of independent governments has frequently run up against the opposing interests of other states no less anxious for stability but wary of the risks inherent in outside interference to achieve it. Finally, as the concept of "calculated" interests implies, interests present under some circumstances (that is, at certain times or in accordance with local political conditions) may diminish or disappear under other circumstances. This seems the proper juncture to state that the specific policy recommendations which flow from the interest analysis presented in this section are not meant to be binding over the ten-year time frame; quite the contrary, the stress here is on the need for greater flexibility in assumptions and policy formulations to take account of diversity in the politics and foreign policies of Southeast Asian governments, whether they be now hostile, friendly, or nonaligned.

defense of the United States; (2) economic—those re-sources, actual or potential, which are essential to the well-being of American society or which, in the hands of a hostile power, would be seriously detrimental to the United States; (3) historical-psychological—those special considerations which have arisen out of long-standing friendly association and which thereby impose certain moral obligations on the United States; (4) political-legal —those official pledges or treaties by which the United States has undertaken particular commitments to foreign governments; and (5) regional peace and stability— those situations or circumstances which promote stabilized relations with major hostile powers in ways which do not compromise security as defined above.

On the basis of these five criteria, the United States has vital interests in seven Asian countries: Japan, the Republic of Korea, Australia–New Zealand, the Philippines, Thailand, and the Republic of China.[8] The precise nature of these interests is examined below.

Japan.   Japan is the major American market in Asia and the major source of American imports from Asia. The Japanese market, compared with global markets for American goods and sources of American imports, has significant value; in 1966, Japan purchased 7 percent of US exports (or about half of all US exports to Asia) and was the source of 10 percent of all US imports (or 67 percent of all US imports from Asia). More important, control by

---

[8] For reasons offered below, Thailand and Nationalist China, although included here as vital interests of the United States, embrace particular defense or political problems which would seem to call for different approaches to protecting those interests than our interests in the other five nations. Japan and Korea, though part of North Asia, are included in the discussion here to help underscore the different kinds of American interests in Asia as well as to serve as points of comparison between interests in Southeast as opposed to North Asia.

a hostile nation of the immense physical and industrial resources of Japan would critically alter the regional and global distribution of power. The economic might of Japan makes it the only Asian nation whose security from enemy control has a direct and immediate bearing on the security of the United States.

Japan also has inestimable political value to the United States. Japan is the primary example in the region of healthy political and economic development under free conditions. The United States, as much through the crucial tutelary role it played during the occupation period as through the 1960 Security Treaty, has an obligation to defend Japan against external aggression and foreign-oriented subversion.

Korea. The importance of Japan's security is the primary, though certainly not the only, reason why the United States also has a strong interest in Korea. Complete Communist control of South Korea would be intolerable from the standpoint of Japanese security interests, might compel full-scale Japanese rearmament, and might again make Korea the locale of a major-power conflict. Independent of the Japanese relationship, moreover, the United States, having become the major guarantor of the Republic of Korea's security, having become closely identified with its economic and political progress, and having committed itself to defense of that nation against external attack under the 1955 treaty, could hardly renounce its obligations without seriously undermining the confidence of other allies in Asia and throughout the world in the value of American friendship.

Australia and New Zealand. The special relationship which the United States enjoys with Australia and New Zealand hardly needs elaboration—nor does the fact of a direct American commitment to defense of these two long-time allies under the Australia–New Zealand–United States (ANZUS) Treaty.

Philippines. Apart from the intertwined political histories of the Philippines and the United States since 1898, and the mutual defense pact of 1951, the island republic has been a major contributor to America's security system in the Far East since the end of World War II. Most recently, President Marcos made a considerable political sacrifice in pushing for a small contribution of noncombat troops to Vietnam. A less-than-military victory in South Vietnam may bring pressure to bear on Marcos from domestic quarters and might even compel some revision of the US-base agreement; but close Philippines-US ties are likely to continue and may even become stronger insofar as they relate to US obligations to defend the islands against external aggression. While that commitment is clear so long as it is wanted, the United States would certainly not be precluded from reassessing other aspects of its relationship with the Philippines should internal developments there make close identification with a particular government or specific programs undesirable.

Thailand. Thailand is a special case because the vital nature of the American interest is not, as in the other cases, embodied in a definitive defense treaty. Nevertheless, the Joint Statement issued by Foreign Minister Thanat Khoman and Secretary Rusk on March 6, 1962, is a strong pledge which communicates the essentials of a firm commitment. In the statement, the United States specifically assured Thailand of its determination to defend that nation against aggression or subversive attack, independent of American obligations under the SEATO Treaty.

The Thanat-Rusk statement is only a partial explanation of the American interest in Thailand. In addition, the United States has enjoyed a lengthy period of friendship with, and closeness to, the Thais which stretches back to the mid-nineteenth century and the reign of King Mongkut. Especially since the end of the World War II, successive American administrations have encouraged various Thai governments in their support of American policies and US efforts in Korea and Vietnam. While it is often said, and probably with considerable justification, that the Thai have no particular ideological affinity for Western democracy, the salient point is that the Thai governments of recent years have, with strong American urging, staked the security of the nation from external attack on the verbal and tangible support of the United States. Thailand's relative vulnerability to Communist military and political pressure, together with the fact that it is neither economically nor strategically indispensable to the United States, may indicate that American commitments there will assume a form substantially different from commitments to other vital interests. Such a possibility would not, however, diminish the essential historical and moral interest of the United States in seeing that so long as Thailand is willing and able it is not dominated by a hostile power.[9]

Republic of China (ROC). The American commitment to Taiwan's defense has been reiterated often since the signing of the bilateral treaty in 1955. Moreover, US political, moral, and economic support for the Nationalist government, first on the mainland and later on Taiwan, would

[9] Domination by a hostile power is used here to mean a forceful seizure of governmental authority by a major alien nation (i.e., China) or an indigenous vanguard party loyal to a hostile foreign power (i.e., the CPT). A Thai move toward neutralism, or a threatened takeover by an indigenous group unfriendly to the United States but not owing allegiance to an enemy power—both at the moment being highly abstract possibilities—are not considered developments inimical to American interests.

make it very difficult to abdicate responsibility for defending the island against external attack. Finally, American officials have consistently proclaimed the island's economic progress to be a model of successful cooperation in foreign development assistance and have frequently encouraged Nationalist ambitions eventually to recover the mainland.

The commitment to Taiwan's defense seems, however, to conflict with the American interest in stabilizing relations with major hostile powers. The United States has a vital interest in working toward a détente with Peking in ways consistent with American security obligations to the ROC. The manner of this revision will be suggested later; suffice it to say that it does seem possible for the United States to begin considering changes in its political relationship with Taipei without having to retract either its commitment to Taiwan's defense or its rarely proclaimed support of the self-determination of the island's people.

To summarize, American interests toward the seven Asian nations discussed above have a number of distinguishing features. In the first place, the American interest is anchored in a bilateral defense treaty or, in the Thailand case, in a bilateral defense pledge. Second, the United States has a lengthy history of intimate involvement with these nations which has led to the creation of strong psychological attachments, feelings of special friendship, and multifaceted ties of a cultural, economic, and political nature. The same cannot be said of American relations with Malaysia, Indonesia, Burma, Laos, Singapore, or Cambodia.[10] Finally, despite the fact that the

[10] At this point it should be emphasized that certain of the nonvital countries could subsequently become vital. Indonesia, for example, could conceivably become a crucial interest of the United States if its immense resource potential were ever sufficiently exploited to create a circumstance where domination of Indonesia by a hostile power would so strengthen that power as to create a clear threat to the United States.

security and economic well-being of the United States would not be critically affected by a hostile takeover of these nations (except for Japan), any more than of other nonvital nations, the seven in question have chosen to, and been encouraged to, identify with American leadership in a variety of ways. The consequences of a withdrawal of the US defense commitment would be traumatic not only for their governments but for American allies outside the region and for other friendly or nonaligned Asian nations which indirectly benefit, in political stability and military security, from the American commitment.

IV

PROBLEMS AND PROSPECTS FOR US INTERESTS IN SOUTHEAST ASIA OVER THE NEXT TEN YEARS

What developments in Southeast Asia during the next decade are most likely to confront the United States with critical policy choices? Of the separate problem areas to be examined, the constraints imposed by domestic pressures in the United States and the British withdrawal from "east of Suez" are two already recognizable developments whose impact can begin to be gauged. For the remaining four—similar problems of development in Southeast Asia; Communist China's internal politics, foreign policies, and nuclear role; Soviet interests in Southeast Asia; and the Japanese role in the region—it is necessary to analyze the past and present to project the future.

American Domestic Constraints

The formulation of future US policies toward Southeast Asia will be strongly influenced by, and the range of choices at least initially restricted by, domestic developments. The present American administration is bound to encounter serious obstacles at home to engaging the nation in activities that may lead to direct military involvement abroad. Competing claims to resources—civil rights, urban affairs, unemployment, etc.—and bipartisan concern that America's house must first be put in order will make it politically risky for legislators to advocate increased military and economic commitments overseas. The sharp reductions in Congress of the administration's fiscal 1969 foreign aid budget requests illustrate the latter point. The same situation would hold true even if a settlement in Vietnam favorable to American-GVN interests were achieved. The exorbitant manpower, money, and domestic political costs of the war will almost certainly reduce the US government's flexibility in the conduct of foreign affairs. Even if so disposed, the present administration will find it much harder to obtain support for making new, and backing without question old, defense obligations in Southeast Asia, especially those that are somewhat ambiguous.

The British Withdrawal

The announcement by Prime Minister Wilson on January 16, 1968, that British forces will be withdrawn from the Far East by the end of 1971 rather than by 1975, as originally planned, introduces further complications. The British move will affect about 52,000 military personnel, 30,000 of whom are stationed in Singapore. Though not a formal withdrawal from SEATO, the British removal will create a gap in the defense of the Malaysia–Singapore and Australia–New Zealand areas.[1] Some Asian nations, partly in response to the British decision, have already called for consultations among the members of the

[1] A more concrete result will be the strain on Singapore's economy, which already must deal with a 10 percent unemployment problem. British bases contribute about 20 percent of Singapore's national income; they directly employ nearly 24,000 civilians. There are, however, promising signs that Singapore will be able to attract new industrial investors and to have economic barriers among the ASEAN members lowered.

ASEAN (Association of South-East Asian Nations) to address problems of post-1971 security. In a different vein, Malaysia has proposed a mutual nonaggression pact with Indonesia and is working out joint air-defense plans with Singapore. The British themselves agreed in June 1969 at Canberra to maintain a ground contingent in Malaysia and to undertake air and naval training in Asian waters, but they emphatically ruled out any commitments to the defense of Malaysia and her neighbors. Taken together, these Asian initiatives and the various limitations on British participation in regional defense after 1971 raise the possibility that the United States will be called upon to undertake part of the British burden. This possibility, in turn, raises problems concerning the response consonant with American interests.

Similar Problems of Development in Southeast Asian Nations

The underdeveloped nations of Southeast Asia share an outlook and problems relevant to future US policy. Among these, three are particularly important: the nature of nationalism, the requirements of economic development, and the transparency of ideology.

The expression of national consciousness has operated on two levels. Within individual countries it has meant the jealous safeguarding of sovereignty, and suspicion of the motivations of all outsiders. Yet minority ethnic and other groups, such as those in Burma and Thailand, inhibit the fullest development of national identity. Indeed, subnationalism, or localism, seems to be a far more serious obstacle to national integration and political modernization than any externally supported revolutionary movement. Nor has the commonality of nationalistic sentiments

43

yet resulted in a uniformly more worldly or region-oriented outlook. For some nations (such as Thailand and Indonesia), a latent desire for regional leadership underlies an interest in regional cooperation, while for others (Burma and Cambodia), fears of compromising individually tailored forms of neutralism create a reluctance to enter into close contact with neighboring countries. Added to these attitudes are the historic conflicts among the states of the region, which seem to have a momentum of their own—as for example in relations between Thailand and Cambodia, Vietnam and Cambodia, and Malaysia and the Philippines. Nationalism is thus not a binding, unifying sentiment, either against neocolonialism or communism, or in favor of pan-Asianism.

Nationalistic sentiments have, however, been generally aroused by the presence of foreign forces and bases. The Vietnam conflict may, as some assert, have bought time for several Southeast Asian nations to recognize a common need for regional association, but this recognition also includes a reaction against all forms of foreign assistance which could become interference. For example, even if the Vietnam conflict should end in a way relatively favorable to the United States, Thai and Filipino concern over the domestic political implications of American bases, and especially the attractive propaganda target they provide for anti-government forces (as in Vietnam), is unlikely to subside. Moreover, the extensiveness of the US base system in Vietnam, and the destructiveness of air power there (quite aside from the question of its contributions to the war effort), may have added to the convictions of allied nations that any American help in their defense must be confined to material assistance.

The nationalistic considerations affecting the issue of military bases may lead to convergent pressure from important allies (such as the Philippines) to reduce the

American deterrent capability in the Far East sooner than circumstances warrant. In the foreseeable future, and especially as Communist China's nuclear potential grows, an American commitment to the defense of key allies against overt aggression necessitates the maintenance of a credible strategic retaliatory capability in the region. For this reason, a modification of existing arrangements on Okinawa, for example, cannot be considered apart from the basing agreements for the Philippines. An adequate balance seems required between the recognition of the political drawbacks to foreign bases and the function they serve—principally, to remind allies and enemies alike of America's continuing obligations in the area and thus to prevent a miscalculation of the US commitment. Consequently, certain issues will have to be confronted and reassessed: the kind of deterrence rationale appropriate to the security threat in Southeast Asia, the effect new technological advances (such as Poseidon missiles launched from Polaris submarines) will have on land-base requirements, and the point at which a given base becomes more a political liability than a military advantage.

The Southeast Asian nations have taken widely divergent paths in their economic development. The most successful, such as Thailand, Malaysia, and the Philippines, have increased gross national products, but the benefits of prosperity, aided by foreign assistance and investment, have been so unevenly distributed that all three countries still face internal unrest of varying magnitudes. In Indonesia, on the other hand, the failure of political leadership to impose economic discipline has produced chaos in both the industrial and the monetary systems—a chaos that only recently has begun to be rectified. Moreover, the region's governments are hampered by the typical problem of finding an appropriate balance between industrialization and agriculture: in industrializing, they lack entrepreneurial skills and savings for investment, both of which are often dominated by overseas Chinese; in promoting agriculture, they face competitive markets within and without their own region which cause unpredictable fluctuations in the prices of their primary product exports. All of these difficulties are compounded by unchecked population growth. Finally, in the few cases where educational systems have proved able to produce skilled technicians in abundance, the economies have been unable to absorb them. As a result, either the familiar brain drain to the West is accelerated or local unemployment problems are compounded.

In spite of these problems, it is an obvious but often overlooked point that these nations have a great capacity for survival built on tremendous pride of achievement. In the past their problems were frequently alluded to as those of "broken-backed societies."[2] Yet these nations have managed somehow to weather international and domestic crises which by any sophisticated calculation would have seemed insurmountable. Perhaps the lesson is that these nations' claims to sovereignty, their intention to defend it, and their cyclical upheavals in the process of implementing it need to be looked at outside the framework of traditional Cold-War analysis. This is not to argue that they do not desire and should not be offered a helping hand. Rather, it is to suggest that the regenerative and productive powers of the nations of Southeast Asia (and elsewhere) seem far greater than is often appreciated. There are implications here for US foreign aid programs —specifically, the consideration of the way they may be made more compatible with Asian nationalism, with a growing conviction of the value of interdependence, and with a common suspicion of political strings.

[2] A thought-provoking essay on this point has been written by Hugh Tinker as the introduction to his *Re-Orientations: Essays on Asia in Transition* (New York: Frederick A. Praeger, 1965).

The extraordinary resilience of the region's nations is far more apparent than are the ideological affinities of their governments. The experience of the United States during the 1960s in attempting to work with assertedly pro-Western, anti-Communist governing elites in Laos and South Vietnam illustrates the distinction. One of the principal grounds for American involvement there was that pro-Western governments were being threatened by forces dedicated to Communist ideals. In retrospect, it is highly questionable whether the United States should support regimes solely or primarily on the basis of their claims of allegiance to the West and aversion to communism. In Laos, Vietnam, and nearly everywhere else in Southeast Asia, ideological leanings seem primarily to be functions of competition over personal or organizational power. Again, where the framework of Cold-War analysis is adopted, the question too often posed in crisis situations is what the "loss" of a given nation will mean to the regional or global Communist–non-Communist balance of power. In actuality, the political forces in Southeast Asia do not seem to be engaged in a struggle of competing ideologies, certainly not of a kind that conforms to Western images of right versus left, democratic versus nondemocratic, closed versus pluralistic.

Remembering the discussion of the American national interest in Southeast Asia, therefore, two points seem especially important. First, American support of a government on the basis of a perceived goal-identity (the obstruction of Communist influence) ignores the fundamental point that most of these governments consistently base their political allegiances on shifts in the relations between the major powers rather than on a commitment to any distinctive set of ideological tenets. Second, United States efforts to use its support to induce Southeast Asian political institutions and practices to become more compatible with its democratist preferences are likely to fail. This is

47

not due solely to the historic absence of such conceptions (outside Oceania). It is also because the partner government rarely accepts cooperation against communism in order to implement democracy.

Communist China

Internal Politics and External Policy. The scope of political changes within China will naturally be most critically influenced by jockeying for position within the leadership following Mao's death or removal from the scene. Until that time, Mao's continuation in power makes predictions about the Cultural Revolution hazardous, particularly since Mao is quite capable of reversing the ebbing of the revolution that has been going on since September 1967. Mao's political style seems to accept the inevitability of contradictions throughout the society; and since China is still in a political transition, he apparently regards a cycle of ideological reformation campaigns as necessary to ensure that contradictions do not become "antagonistic" and lead to unmanageable conflict.

The unprecedented turmoil of the Cultural Revolution, however, may have imposed certain restraints on Mao's freedom to plunge into revolution again. While the question of whether Mao exercises full decision-making power cannot be answered, it does seem reasonable to suppose that the army, because of its dominant role in national politics since early 1967, and Chou En-lai, whose influence evidently carries considerable weight with Mao, will find a common interest in making the restoration of political and economic order the government's primary task for the new few years. The army and Chou may cooperate, in other words, to channel extremism in relatively harmless directions. The declining importance of the Red Guards whom the regime has apparently found an increasingly intolerable burden, is one sign that ideological fanaticism is losing favor, if only because it has served its purpose.

If a period of consolidation sets in, as would appear to have been ordained by the Ninth Communist Party Congress of April 1969, it seems fairly certain to be a lengthy one, regardless of whether the reins of power are primarily in military, party, or Mao's hands. The probability at the moment is that the military will at least initially dominate the political scene because it has been vested with authority to set up revolutionary committees. How long the army might be prepared to rule and be capable of ruling, and to what extent it would be willing to share power with nonmilitary leaders or to tolerate a revitalization of the Chinese Communist Party (CCP), would then become key questions. In such a transitional period, the Chinese political system would encompass governing institutions of varying composition depending on the local power situation (the vitality of the party, the willingness of political cadres to risk becoming part of the power structure again, the strength and prestige of local military commanders, etc.). Inasmuch as the CCP has been seriously weakened because of the Cultural Revolution,[3] with demoralization doubtless widespread in the party's ranks at all levels, and since some military leaders will find political power to their liking (a phenomenon common to other underdeveloped nations where the military has come to power for the first time), the army can be expected to retain a formidable share of political influence for some time to come.

Whatever the organizational form through which the army seeks to exert that influence, however, and whichever combination of local-central power relationship

[3] Regarding the present and future circumstances of the CCP, see Charles Neuhauser, "The Impact of the Cultural Revolution on the Chinese Communist Party Machine," *Asian Survey*, vol. VIII, no. 6 (June 1968), pp. 465–88.

evolves, two major outcomes may be anticipated: first, a lengthy period of domestic uncertainty in China, dominated by Peking's efforts to assert its legitimacy and authority over the provinces and perhaps punctuated by violent struggles over the boundaries of political and economic autonomy; and, second, even with Mao's passing, a resiliency in Chinese political institutions sufficient to accommodate this kind of competition without precipitating civil war or widespread political violence.

Under a second set of circumstances, Mao's demise or effective removal from authority (such as his being made figurehead party chairman) could precipitate a massive hemorrhage of the Chinese political system leading to a breakdown of central authority and the emergence of warlord-like satrapies. This possibility would depend in large part on a substantial diminution of army control to the point where it would be incapable of preventing widespread convulsions. It implies that other power sources exist to challenge the army or to induce substantial segments of it to defy central authority. Although such a possibility cannot be excluded, it is unlikely, for while Mao's eclipse might well spark competition over his successor, present events make the above assumptions about the diffuseness and fragility of the army's power debatable. In a sense, political events in China during 1968—including the return of some first- and second-rank party officials to their posts—may be seen as establishing a new, army-sanctioned order for the post-Mao period while Mao is still around.

In the event of a rather extensive breakdown of central authority, China's foreign relations would be frozen. China's claims to revolutionary leadership and prestige would then have little credence, and Peking-supported revolutionary parties would find themselves isolated. But this contingency is neither as analytically interesting nor as relevant as the foreign policy of a leadership that may shift in composition but will retain relative stability. If nations learn from their mistakes—and China's retrenchment in the fall of 1967 would seem to suggest that it does —then it is more probable that China will maintain a moderate foreign policy than that, under the impact of internal political competition, it will be susceptible to alternating periods of "lashing out" and "looking inward."

The alternative—a militant China which, under strong army influence or domination, might probe India's defenses, might be more inclined to support revolutionary Communist movements across the frontiers, or might seek to wrest disputed territory from the Soviet Union—seems improbable. First, an army-backed or army-led leadership might have a strong interest in ameliorating relations with the Soviet Union in order to satisfy the People's Liberation Army's (PLA) modernization needs, to improve defense against external attack, and to prevent the Soviet Union from taking advantage of China's internal unrest. Second, the Chinese Communist armed forces have always been primarily defense oriented, whether in the air or on the ground. Maoist military doctrine has consistently stressed China's need to maintain a capability to wipe out the ground invasion that must inevitably follow an enemy air-naval attack. Moreover, the accusations which followed the purge of General Lo Jui-ch'ing indicate that the central issue in dispute was the politicization of the armed forces and Lo's alleged determination to put the army's material needs on a par with ideological training.[4] Foreign policy issues have at best been peripheral to the intra-army confrontation, except in the sense that Lo may have accepted the necessity of a very limited Sino-Soviet rapprochement to bolster Chinese security against an expansion of the Vietnam war. There is little evidence, in

[4] For a more detailed discussion, see Ralph L. Powell, "Maoist Military Doctrines," *Asian Survey*, vol. VIII, no. 4 (April 1968), pp. 239–62.

brief, to support the view that the PLA, and Lin Piao in particular, is any more eager than China's political leaders to engage in foreign adventures; in fact, the Chinese army leadership may be more accurately described as unusually sensitive to the dangers of taking risks abroad.

A continuation of a moderate Chinese foreign policy would mean that priority would be given to the solution of pressing domestic problems, while low-cost external ventures would be confined to the extension of political and material support to anti-imperialist, anti-reactionary governments and pro-Communist movements. Basic Chinese objectives would not be fundamentally altered. The chief difference between future and past policy would probably lie in the new regime's greater sensitivity to developments abroad,[5] including, perhaps, initiatives from the United States and the Soviet Union. A less radical, less ideologically burdened leadership might slowly emerge that would not only concentrate on reestablishing China's image as upholder of the Bandung spirit but might also be capable of reacting more realistically and flexibly to the non-Communist world.

Taiwan. The composition of the next Chinese leadership and the shape of government organization on the mainland are almost certain not to affect Peking's attitude toward

[5] One indication of this sensitivity was given in late November 1968 when Peking proposed to Washington a resumption of the Warsaw talks on February 20, 1969. Although Peking cancelled the talks at the last moment, it is still important to speculate on China's motivations in having originally requested them. Generally speaking, Peking was no doubt interested in assessing the new Administration's attitude. But Peking's primary motivation may have been to undermine what appears as "Soviet-American collusion" over Vietnam and Southeast Asia generally. By demonstrating a willingness to talk to the Americans, the CPR may have hoped to convince other nations of its moderateness, to provoke Soviet agitation over a possible Sino-American détente, and perhaps even to seek to influence the Paris talks now that Hanoi is committed to negotiating.

Taiwan. The Taiwan Strait will therefore unquestionably remain an area of potential danger, the more so if American policy toward China does not significantly change. No Communist Chinese leader, however "moderate" in comparison with his predecessors, is likely to be interested in a compromise solution to the Taiwan problem while American forces continue to "occupy" the island and, more important, while American policy precludes recognition of the mainland regime as the only true representative of the Chinese people.

Insofar as the defense of Taiwan is concerned, the fact that forces of the Republic of China are large (roughly 600,000 counting all services) and that the strait area is so inherently volatile means that US military support will be required there. After a US withdrawal from Vietnam, ROC leverage on the United States will not be so great as, for example, that of Korea or Thailand; no matter how much criticism the Nationalist government levels at an unsatisfactory Vietnam outcome, Taipei cannot risk estranging itself from the United States and providing Washington with a pretext for implementing alternative political ("two Chinas") and military support programs. Nevertheless, Taiwan (like South Korea and Thailand) will represent a continuing dollar drain and, in the wake of unfavorable events in Vietnam, may also request reaffirmation of the American defense obligation.

Sino-Soviet Relations. For the duration of Mao's tenure in power, Sino-Soviet relations are extremely unlikely to improve, and in fact may approach a complete breakdown.[6] Such a breakdown, perhaps encompassing a severance of diplomatic relations, trade ties, and even abrogation of the 1950 mutual defense treaty, could be precipitated by

[6] This section has benefited considerably from an unpublished paper by Arnold Horelick on alternative Sino-Soviet relationships in the 1970s.

hostile incidents (e.g., continuing maltreatment of Chinese officials or students in Moscow, or further flare-ups along the Sino-Soviet border), or by a conviction on the part of the ruling Cultural Revolution group under Mao that China's ideological purity can only be fully clarified by a total rupture in relations with the Moscow revisionists. The foreign policy implications of such a rupture would probably include: (1) no joint Sino-Soviet actions, as is presently the case; (2) renunciation or lapse of the mutual defense treaty in 1980; (3) intensified competition for the allegiance of Communist parties, Communist nations, and nonaligned states; (4) an increased possibility of overt hostilities along the Sino-Soviet frontier, requiring a diversion of Chinese military resources (including, perhaps, strategic capabilities) to those areas; (5) enhanced prospects for further steps in a Soviet-American détente, or possibilities for US initiatives toward China (or both); and (6) an increasing potentiality for a "soft-sell" Chinese approach to Southeast and North Asia which would seek to compensate for lost Soviet trade and aid and would recognize, as the consequence of prospects for border trouble with the Russians, the limitations on Chinese assistance of certain "people's wars."[7]

An entirely different kind of Sino-Soviet relationship might well arise out of an evolution in the Chinese politi-

---

[7] Should Sino-Soviet relations remain roughly comparable to what they are now under Mao, at least 3 points to 6 would still be likely results. This kind of tenuous stabilization could move toward a limited rapprochement after Mao's passing or could result in an open break under circumstances such as those indicated. The possibilities for joint Sino-Soviet actions (point 1) would remain low; but, as Vietnam demonstrated, an unrecognized division of labor amounting to tacit cooperation could come about if US actions on the China periphery led to a major Asian crisis in which the Soviets and the Chinese deemed some kind of cooperation imperative to defend their respective national interests. Finally, the question of the mutual defense treaty's relevance (point 2) could not be so easily dismissed.

cal system. Whether this evolution entails a revival of the CCP, a large military involvement in political decision-making, or rule by a collegium, a principal result might be a limited rapprochement between the two powers. In broad outline, this *modus vivendi*, stemming from the Peking leadership's reassessment of China's military and economic needs, would halt open CPR-USSR polemical attacks, keep the alliance one of equals, and open up possibilities for certain types of mutually advantageous bargains. China would hope to see trade ties strengthened and long-term credit offered. Certain kinds of strategic materials (such as oil, manufactured parts, and defensive weapons and equipment) might be requested by China, but if the Soviets supplied these, they would probably still hold back on sophisticated weapons and aircraft and might impose a ceiling on the level of credit. China would certainly wish to ensure that any Soviet military assistance would not compromise unfettered Chinese control over the weapons.

In return for these benefits, China would probably have to accept the fact that Moscow will continue promoting the Soviet image in Asia. In particular, China would have to refrain from assailing any Soviet efforts to cultivate trade and diplomatic relations with "pro-imperialist" bourgeois regimes (such as Thailand, Malaysia, Singapore, and the Philippines) or to compete with China and the United States for the attention and support of non-Communist, anti-imperialist countries such as Burma, Indonesia, and Cambodia. The Soviets would probably also insist that China cease interfering in East European bloc affairs and uncritically accept Soviet policy there.

China as a Nuclear Power. The rapprochement, however, unquestionably would be limited by the mutual distrust generated in previous years; and one manifestation might be China's continued caution over becoming in-

55

volved in war-risk situations that could compel reliance on the 1950 treaty. China would probably seek to persuade the outside world that deterrence of the United States had been substantially strengthened. Meanwhile the CPR would surely continue working toward the acquisition of an alternative to the Soviet umbrella: a nuclear weapons arsenal and delivery system comprising intermediate-range and eventually intercontinental missiles. It appears that the Chinese have been and will continue to be motivated to develop a completely independent strategic capability, not out of an intention to use nuclear weapons to achieve revolutionary aims, but for prestige, deterrence, and defense reasons. Like other developing nations, China views nuclear weapons as unmistakable evidence of having achieved developed-nation status. Moreover, nuclear weapons would reconfirm to the Chinese their traditional self-assessments of China's historic right to great-power rank.

Prestige is not the only consideration. China's possession of a strategic capability against Asian and eventually a few west-coast American cities—a development clearly foreseeable within the next decade—will give Peking a nascent deterrent to possible US attack. Chinese leaders, military or civilian, would probably consider unlikely the possibility of an unprovoked American attack on China, although they would remain appreciative of American retaliatory power in the event China should commit overt aggression. These considerations, however, would not inhibit Peking from seeking to exploit nuclear weapons to undermine the confidence of America's allies in the willingness of the United States to take risks on their behalf. With at least an MRBM capability, the CPR would be in a position to argue that it has rendered the American nuclear umbrella obsolete and exposed Southeast Asian nations requesting American military intervention in their behalf to the risk of escalation to nuclear warfare. Once

China has acquired a genuine nuclear option, nations of Southeast Asia and Japan will have to take more seriously Peking's contention that they must reconsider the virtues of association with the American security system.[8]

For the United States, then, the key questions to be addressed are, first, whether the Communist threat would be materially raised by a limited Sino-Soviet rapprochement; second, what steps can be taken toward reducing, deflecting, or exploiting the strengths and weaknesses of this kind of relationship; and finally, what strategic posture and political responses seem appropriate in view of China's objectives in developing an independent nuclear force.

The Soviet Role in Southeast Asia

At bottom, the post-Vietnam role of the Soviet Union in Asia will unfold within the larger context of developments in Sino-Soviet and Soviet-American relations. It seems reasonable to conclude, however, that Russia, in consonance with its increasingly global concerns, will read the lessons of Vietnam as calling for greater involvement in Asian affairs than in the Khrushchev era. The Soviets might draw this conclusion from one or more of the following considerations: (1) their tardiness in making material commitments to Hanoi's war effort (February 1965, at the time of Kosygin's visit) may have helped to keep their influence over the course of events at a significantly lower level than would have been the case had they made an earlier display of support and not tacitly accepted a Chinese monopoly of war-related assistance and advice to

[8] On these points, see Alice Langley Hsieh's statement before the Subcommittee on Military Applications of the Joint Committee on Atomic Energy, November 7, 1967, in *Communist China's Military Policies and Nuclear Strategy* (Santa Monica, Calif.: The RAND Corporation, Paper P-3730, November 1967).

the DRV; (2) the United States, whatever the outcome in Vietnam, may again challenge the Soviet position among nonaligned and fraternal socialist nations by intervening in third-world local wars, making it important for Moscow to develop a more flexible military posture either to provide rapid assistance to allies or to introduce the threat of Soviet assistance into American calculations (supporting arguments for these two points would come from the Soviet experience in the June 1967 Arab-Israeli war); (3) Communist China's influence in Southeast Asia has markedly declined since the Cultural Revolution began, and the "democratic, anti-imperialist" forces of the area should have an alternative to both the United States and China; (4) a settlement of the Vietnam war (certainly if through negotiations) will be plausibly claimed as a victory for Soviet diplomacy and consequently an opportunity for promoting the Soviet image in Southeast Asia; (5) in the event of a US-China rapprochement, or of worsening Sino-Soviet relations, the acquisition of positions of strength (political, economic, or military) in Southeast Asia could measurably enchance the Soviets' tactical position toward either or both those powers.[9]

The establishment of diplomatic relations with Malaysia (March 1967) and Singapore (June 1968), at a time when Moscow already had a substantial investment in Indonesia, was a sign that the Soviets were no

[9] Some, if not all, of these elements were present in Soviet Party Secretary Brezhnev's speech of June 7, 1969, in which he referred obliquely to "creating a system of collective security in Asia." Though probably intended as a trial balloon, other Soviet references to collective security before and after Brezhnev's speech indicated a top-level determination to respond to increased foreign-policy flexibility among Southeast Asian governments at a time of declining Chinese influence and prospective American disengagement. Peking was probably close to the mark in interpreting the speech as concrete evidence of a region-wide Soviet effort to contain China—adding that the Soviets expected the Americans and the Japanese to go along.

longer interested in confining their area of concern to the Indian subcontinent. Moreover, quiet Russian diplomacy has gained Moscow small but potentially useful footholds in Burma and Cambodia, and Soviet trade and diplomatic relations with the Philippines seem in the offing. Moscow may, moreover, be eager to expand trade and political contacts with Thailand. Finally, under the impact of Vietnam and a reduced budget for strategic forces, the Soviet military may push for greater flexibility for remote war contingencies by budgeting for naval carrier task forces, more and bigger helicopters, and air-mobile divisions.[10] Determining which of these many moves might be threatening and which could be useful in Asian economic development is a major problem the United States will have to confront.

Moscow may anticipate that better opportunities for eroding the American and Chinese positions in Asia are available in Japan. The Japanese are evidently interested in recent Soviet advances on the northern islands and on the development of Siberia, inasmuch as there lies the way for Japan to broaden its economic involvement in central Asia and eastern Europe. Ultimately, Japan may consider exploiting a US-Soviet détente for such political benefits as the return of the Kurile Islands or even the concluding of a peace treaty with Moscow.

The Soviets, meanwhile, may view closer relations with Japan in terms of acquiring political and economic leverage to induce increased Japanese independence from the United States. While it is debatable whether the Soviets actually consider Japan's neutralization a realistic objective within the next decade, Moscow certainly has an in-

[10] Early indications of a Soviet interest in moving in this direction are surveyed and analyzed in Thomas W. Wolfe, *The Soviet Quest for More Globally Mobile Deterrent Power* (Santa Monica, Calif.: The RAND Corporation, Research Memorandum RM-5554-PR, December 1967).

terest in doing all it can to move Japan in that direction (and thus to deny China the benefits of Japanese trade and possibly aid as well). The Soviets may also desire to bring Japan deeper into the development of resource-rich, sparsely populated Siberia to reduce Japan's economic dependence on the United States and to open up an area potentially vulnerable to Chinese subversion—an effort which Peking has already labeled a Russo-Japanese conspiracy against Chinese territory. The question clearly posed for the United States is whether Soviet-Japanese collaboration in Siberia, or limited political agreements, necessarily compromise the American-Japanese relationship.

Japan and Southeast Asia

Unlike the Soviet Union or the United States, both of which have certain irreducible obligations deriving from their great-power status, Japan so far is free to decide the kind and extent of its involvement in Southeast Asia. Japan's approach to that region has been marked by a discriminating selection of trade and aid partners and by a conscious determination to limit associations. On the one hand, Japan recognizes Southeast Asia's present and potential importance for its economic well-being and business profit. On the other, the Japanese government has repeatedly shown itself uninterested in the region merely for altruistic or prestige purposes, while acknowledging its technological and financial needs. Nor does Japan seem to consider its own security to be intimately intertwined with stability in Southeast Asia, although Tokyo understands the importance to some of the nations there of joining together for their own defense.

Motivated by prospects of profit, Japan's main ties are to Australia and New Zealand, which, as stable, developed nations, are dependable markets. Among the underdeveloped nations, Japan is principally interested in the economic potential of Indonesia. Tokyo, however, has been reluctant to meet Djakarta's requests fully, apparently out of considerable uncertainty about Indonesia's economic and political future. Toward Indonesia as toward most of the other countries of the region, Japan maintains a policy of tying bilateral assistance to the purchase of Japanese goods and of offering loans on comparatively stringent terms. Besides lacking capital, the Japanese are probably anxious to avoid laying too much emphasis on bilateral assistance programs because they are concerned not to appear as exploiters and because they foresee the time when business interests may become so large as to create pressures for government protection of them. These considerations perhaps account in part for Tokyo's willingness to provide funds on a multilateral basis, e.g., through the Asian Development Bank and to Indonesia in combination with other Western nations.

At a time when American assistance programs worldwide will be undergoing a retrenchment, Japan theoretically should be able to take up the slack in Southeast Asia. Japan is the one partner in Asia who not only benefits economically from the security provided by the regionwide American presence but also is capable of paying a major share of the costs. Japan, for example, is especially concerned that the Straits of Malacca, through which must pass approximately 90 percent of its Middle East oil needs, always be kept open. Barring dramatic domestic political changes to the far right, however, it seems fairly clear that Japan will not undertake any of the burden of assuring either with money or manpower—much less with a naval fleet of its own—that the straits remain open to all traffic.

The outlook of the next decade does not promise much beyond what Japan is now doing. Assuming that no basic

61

change occurs in Japan's political orientation or perception of Southeast Asia's relevance to economic and defense needs, Japanese policy will probably continue to avoid deep involvement in an area of constant political and economic uncertainty. Concretely, this means, first, that Tokyo will regard negatively any move by its Southeast Asia partners in ASPAC (Asia and Pacific Council) to transform the organization into a SEATO-like, anti-Communist alliance having, or purporting to have, security functions. Second, Japan will continue to choose carefully among the region's nations for business situations with profit potential. For instance, Tokyo may prove hesitant to underwrite (through the Overseas Economic Development Fund) business ventures in Singapore, where the need for foreign investment will be especially great after 1971, but may be more flexible if the Indonesian economy shows signs of stabilizing. Third, yen credit arrangements are likely to remain the cornerstone of Japanese aid agreements, although Japan may begin loosening up on interest and repayment terms. Finally, Japan may become more receptive to making greater use of multilateral financial institutions, though such a trend would probably depend on American leadership.

In sum, the prospects are for Japan to continue a cautious, discriminating approach to Southeast Asia. In a period during which several fundamental aspects of the Japanese–American alliance will be undergoing intensive reassessment, Washington's ability to induce a greater Japanese commitment to Southeast Asia's development is likely to be very limited. To the degree that Japan can be influenced, as will be suggested later, much may depend on the extent of the United States' own involvement.

V

TOWARD AN AMERICAN POLICY FOR THE NEXT DECADE

In view not only of the different challenges likely to be posed by China and North Vietnam in the next decade but also of the distinctive security environments which exist in areas of special concern to the United States in Southeast Asia, different kinds and levels of American commitments will be required. No single doctrine seems adequate to guide American policy in areas either of vital or of secondary interests. The recommendations below, first with respect to areas of direct American concern (including Communist China) and then to nations of secondary concern, are offered with a view to accommodating the wide range of changing internal and external conditions within the Southeast Asia region in ways that will permit the United States to preserve its immediate and long-range interests there.

In broad outline (the details are set forth below), a set of policies the United States might retain or adopt, and courses of action it might follow, are listed here:

1. undertake no new bilateral or multilateral defense obligations, in the belief that the American commitment to the security of vital allies from hostile external domination is sufficient under existing treaties or pledges;

2. reaffirm where necessary existing commitments to specific countries, but seek to accommodate to anticipated

evolutionary trends in American relations with the Philippines, Thailand, and perhaps Australia by being flexible should pressures arise to reduce the American presence;

3. retain a credible air and sea capacity in the western Pacific as a deterrent against (highly unlikely) nuclear attack or overt aggression, and demonstrate a continuing American concern for regional security through periodic show-the-flag maneuvers involving all services under SEATO auspieces;

4. approach very cautiously any requests for assistance from new Asian military organizations which might be established;

5. couple changes in the political substance of relations with Taiwan to important modifications of the present diplomatic posture toward Communist China (a one-Taiwan, one-China formula);

6. reappraise priorities and funding alternatives for military and economic assistance, giving particular attention to multilateral institutions as alternatives to bilateral programs;

7. examine ways in which Soviet involvement in the region can be accommodated within the range of presently or potentially available economic mechanisms;

8. rely on diplomatic initiatives to try to ease Communist pressures on Laos and Cambodia, accepting the prevailing military balance and its political implications in Laos as well as Cambodia's need to orient its neutralism around Hanoi's policies and actions.

Policies toward Vital Areas of US Interest

Australia and New Zealand. Australian and New Zealand disappointment at a US "failure" in Vietnam would be unlikely to weaken significantly the close ties of the ANZUS nations. Barring unforeseen dramatic political changes, the security alignment of the two nations is virtually inevitable.

It would be wrong, however, to preclude the possibility of important modifications in the relationship among the ANZUS partners. Within the next decade, for instance, the feasibility and desirability of US missile, nuclear submarine, or strategic bomber bases in Australia may become major topics of public dialogue. A reduction of US bases in the Philippines, or China's entry into a new phase of belligerent action, could provide the occasion for official consideration of such questions—which have already become part of the strategic debate in Australia. As one example, Professor Hedley Bull, whose views on the implications of a limited US involvement in Asia for Australian security have been cited previously, has argued that the best guarantee of a continuing American commitment to his nation's defense after Vietnam lies in persuading the United States to establish bases on Australian soil. Even if that step should entail some cost to Australia's diplomatic independence, he contends, the benefits to Australia of creating a greater American stake there would make the bargain worthwhile. Bull's primary concern is to bolster continental defense; but while he concedes that Australia may have to provide some temporary military assistance to Malaysia and Singapore after the British withdrawal, the logical extreme of his position, "Fortress Australia," is probably receiving serious consideration too. With that, the possibility that Australia, either in cooperation with New Zealand or independently, would decide to develop its own nuclear capability could not be excluded.

As China's nuclear development progresses, and perhaps as overriding political considerations compel a reduction in American bases in Japan (including Okinawa) and the Philippines, the attractiveness of strategic bomber or missile bases in Australia may increase. Viewed from the

American standpoint, however, the arguments against accepting base facilities in Australia, should they be offered
(which itself is still a questionable point), sound more
persuasive. Any Australian request would probably derive
directly from uncertainty about the American commitment
in extremis rather than because of immediate concern
about the Chinese nuclear threat. By reaffirming existing
bilateral treaties, perhaps while specifying unilateral guarantees against nuclear attack,[1] the United States should
be able to undercut Australian opinion that only a direct
American presence can assure the American commitment.
At the same time, of course, it would seem prudent to
avoid making statements or taking actions that might
exaggerate the nuclear danger to Southeast Asia, such as
offering support for a regional ABM system to substitute
for or augment additional US land bases.

If the American commitment is restated with firmness,
it seems unlikely that in the coming decade an Australian
government would want to risk the domestic repercussions
of inviting a US military presence that would make
Oceania a strategic enemy target for the first time. United
States intercontinental missiles, unlike strategic bombers,
would have a certain deterrent value, of course; but it remains highly questionable whether an Australian government would be able to push through a missile-base program in the name of deterrence without considerable
evidence that the power to be deterred—Communist
China—represents a clear and present danger. Despite
opposition from such strategists as Bull, therefore, Australia may find it more in its defense interests to seek

---

[1] Australia, like most other nations in the region, is probably
dubious about American pledges of retaliation couched in terms
of the Tri-Nation (US-UK-USSR) Security Council resolution
of June 1968, which promises protection for non-nuclear-weapon
states against the threat of or actual attack by nuclear-weapon
states (i.e., China).

military cooperation or nonaggression agreements with neighboring countries whose defense bears more immediately on Australian security. Especially if Great Britain can provide some assistance—and the Canberra talks of June 1969 indicate that limited British cooperation can be expected—the security of Oceania should be greatly advanced under arrangements which the United States could support at relatively low cost.

Philippines. As elsewhere in Southeast Asia, in the Philippines the Vietnam war has had the twin effects of underlining the need for more concerted efforts at regional collaboration and of demonstrating the political risks of identifying too closely with American policies. Political opposition is already mounting—and, in the wake of an unfavorable outcome in Vietnam, should become more pronounced—for a loosening or restructuring of ties to the United States. A growing number of young intellectuals and politicians—including two of the most prominent members of the opposition Liberal Party, Antonio Villegas (the dynamic mayor of Manila) and Joirto Salonga—have already begun to stress the need for greater Philippine independence from the United States.

Accentuated expressions of Filipino nationalism will no doubt focus on the base issue, which promises to be the most pressing of several problems in US-Philippine relations during the next decade. The accomplished fact of the reduction of the base lease to 25 years need not, however, mean that the Philippine government is bound to demand abrogation of it. But domestic political considerations may well lead it to insist that certain nonessential US naval and air facilities be eliminated, or to request the start of negotiations for more favorable arrangements on such base-related matters as customs duties and the SOFA (Status-of-Forces Agreement). Manila remains aware of the economic and military importance of the major US facilities (Clark Air Base and the naval base at Subic Bay), an importance that will be underlined in the event the Okinawa complex must be reduced or abandoned. If Okinawa can be retained, on the other hand, it would seem possible and, in the long view, desirable that the United States maintain a flexible position when it comes to negotiating the base question. As with Japan and the problem of US bases on Okinawa and the home islands, American sensitivity to the home government's domestic political problems in confronting the base issue (as well as such other politically volatile questions as the sugar quota) will probably do more to ensure a lasting partnership through compromise than will a rigid stance that runs counter to prevailing popular opinion.

Differences over President Marcos' strong stand in support of American policies in Vietnam and over the character of Filipino-American relations have been only the most publicized manifestations of divisiveness in Filipino politics. Broadly speaking, the chronic instability of politics in the island republic should be as much a matter of concern to the United States as the particular issues relating to foreign policy. Specifically, the United States, in weighing the value of basing rights in the Philippines, may want to consider the inordinate amount of corruption and gangsterism which characterizes so much of present-day political life there. Circumstances such as those indicated above, which force the Philippine government to modify the relationship in response to criticism of its subordination to American policy, may actually provide an opportunity for the United States to become less closely identified with a progressive-minded but politically insecure government.

In a similar vein—although the rebellion of the Hukbalahap, which persists mainly in central Luzon where it began twenty years ago, has not reached dramatic proportions—no American commitment to assist in suppressing the rebellion would seem warranted. For the foreseeable future, the Philippine government is unlikely to make such a request. But considering the worst case, the contention here is that in the Philippines, as in Thailand and Burma, the predominant responsibility for counteracting the rebel forces rests with the indigenous government. The Huk guerrillas are likely to expand their territory and strength only as the hinterlands in which they operate continue to be given secondary attention by Manila. There is, however, considerable evidence that land reform and related measures are being implemented by the Marcos government and that the insurgent organization, lacking a sanctuary or outside assistance, can be contained.

Thailand. Regardless of the outcome within Vietnam, the Thais will surely want to know precisely where they stand with relation to US security planning for Southeast Asia. Concerned primarily with Communist ambitions in Laos, the RTG will probably be particularly interested in eliciting explicit American positions on these issues: (1) the US commitment—the extent to which the United States can be counted on, especially under a new administration, to provide continued assurances against overt aggression, however remote either side may presently consider the contingency; (2) Vietnam-related war materiel—the disposition of American aircraft based in Thailand during the Vietnam conflict; and, (3) the military and economic aid program—the effects of AID cutbacks on US programs for Thailand, especially those having direct relevance to the counterinsurgency program.

The fact that the United States enjoys a special relationship with Thailand need not imply that US policy, and particularly US commitments, must be shaped by the actions and demands of Bangkok. One of the most disturbing aspects of the US-RTG relationship since the early 1950s has been the excessive availability of American political, economic, and military support to successive Thai governments. What leverage the United States acquired through such support might have been used to prevent the Thai military from using US aid to consolidate the army's dominant political position. Instead, American influence has frequently been undercut by the Thai government's thinly veiled threats to "go neutral," to reduce political and military ties to the Western alliance, and to "accommodate" to major Communist powers. The 1962 Thanat-Rusk statement, in fact, arose precisely out of strong hints from Bangkok, during heavy fighting across the Laotian border, that a major reappraisal of Thailand's foreign policy might have to be made unless the United States became committed unilaterally to Thai security.

Most clearly in the wake of a Vietnam settlement that would leave the Viet Cong in a strong position to take over that country, Thailand might again be faced with a major Communist threat via Laos. RTG spokesmen alluded in 1968 to the possibility of a substantial American withdrawal from Asia after a settlement in Vietnam. Bangkok might, therefore, seek not simply a reaffirmation of the 1962 pledge but a strengthening of it, such as in a formal bilateral defense treaty.[2]

---

[2] Present (and traditional) Thai thinking, however, is that alliances, including those based upon treaties, are only reliable to the extent that the national interests of the allied parties remain compatible. Promises exchanged between allies, whether or not by treaty, may be broken any time circumstances compel one party to reassess its national interests. Thus, a bilateral defense treaty with the United States would no more guarantee Thailand an American commitment than does the 1962 statement; the United States will come to Thailand's assistance because American interests, not paper promises, so dictate. The realism of this position has led Thailand to consider the guarantees made under the draft Nuclear Nonproliferation Treaty and the US-UK-USSR Security Council resolution insufficient and to refuse to sign the treaty. By the same token, the RTG might reverse its position on a defense treaty with the United States if it considered that circumstances after Vietnam required a change.

While it would indeed be unwise for the United States to abandon the 1962 commitment, there would seem little justification for going beyond that into a deeper commitment by treaty. The United States would have to consider that a formal commitment (1) could lead at some future date to a request that US forces, for the first time, help combat the insurgency in the north and the northeast or support a Thai force which might cross the Mekong into Laotian territory to meet a Pathet Lao threat; (2) would give a Thai government, especially if still under primarily military control, even greater leeway to neglect some of the important social and economic bases of unrest and to ignore demands for increased political freedom under the 1968 constitution; and (3) would go a long way toward ensuring the continued dependence of the RTG on the United States at a time when "self-reliance," if actually implemented, would probably be most desirable from the standpoint of both Thai and American interests.

If the Thai government is in fact a firm ally of the United States, it would seem unlikely that an American refusal to offer additional security guarantees would be sufficient cause for a complete reversal of Thai policy. Another display of US hesitancy to come to the assistance of "rightist" and/or "neutralist" forces in Laos should warfare intensify there—coming on the heels of a Vietnam setback and American caution on further commitments to Asian security—would stand a strong chance of forcing Bangkok to reassess existing policies.

A gradual and deliberate Thai dissociation from security links to the United States, however, need not be contrary to the interests of either party. Should the RTG decide that the Americans are not prepared to go beyond diplomacy to prevent a Communist takeover in Laos (which would also increase Communist pressure on Cambodia), the government might decide to reduce

71

participation in SEATO, dilute significantly the anti-Communist tone of its policy statements, expand trade relations with the Soviet Union, or reverse its announced position on all-Asian regional military cooperation, perhaps by spearheading a movement to convert ASEAN into a security organization. Rather than presaging Thai neutralism, however, these steps might be regarded as positive evidence that the RTG is firmly committed to relying on its own resources to fashion its place in Southeast Asia. If the American role in Thailand were thereby reduced to the promise of protection against overt aggression by Chinese or North Vietnamese forces and to the continued provision of economic and military aid, the long-term soundness of the Thai political system might actually be enhanced.

The Communist threat to Thailand would be most unlikely to magnify if such a change in Bangkok's attitude should come to pass. It seems improbable that any Thai government would reduce its attention to the Communist-led insurgent threat as relations with the United States undergo transition. On the contrary, if Thai policy were less dependent on American support, the insurgents would seem more likely to lose the credibility of a major propaganda theme: the charge that the "Thanom-Praphat clique" is no more than a puppet of the American neo-colonialists. The RTG might also be more strongly motivated to devote itself wholeheartedly to the solution of minority problems in the north and to the satisfaction of grievances of its people in the northeast. Although American officials and advisory personnel might then lose some influence over the structure and content of Thai counterinsurgency and related rural development programs, the United States could retain as much influence (which in any case may be more imagined than real) from a comparatively aloof posture toward the RTG as from a position of close interaction with Thai officials at all levels. The insurgent movement is far more likely to become a significant security concern because of RTG ineffectiveness and insensitivity than because of inadequate American support or the inability of American officials to bring their advice to bear.

Lesser Thai dependence on the United States might, on the contrary, improve the chances for Thai security vis-à-vis Communist China. If overt Thai-American military cooperation were sharply reduced, the Chinese might begin to have second thoughts about remaining hostile to Bangkok. Under those circumstances, whether the Chinese chose to continue providing political support to the CPT would probably depend less on that party's announced ideological position than on Thailand's relations with Taiwan (at present unprecedentedly close) and its willingness to reopen questions of cultural and trade contacts left dormant in the mid-1950s.[3] As with the White Flags in Burma, China has a weak ally in the CPT and could, as in the past, either choose to ignore it or merely give it perfunctory verbal attention and enough material support to keep the party alive.

While the United States might, then, make clear the limitations of the American commitment to Thailand's defense—in particular the position that the rebellion can be contained with American assistance to government forces—the RTG will probably request that the United States demonstrate its friendship by augmenting military and economic assistance. Within limits defined by the budget and the Congress, the United States could probably grant military aid increases for insurgency-related, rather

[3] Hesitantly in 1968 and then quite openly early in 1969, Foreign Minister Thanat indicated increased flexibility in his government's attitude toward Communist China. With the proviso that Peking must first adopt a less bellicose posture toward Bangkok, Thanat expressed his preparedness to talk with China's leaders and hinted that Thailand might reconsider its position on a CPR seat in the United Nations and on diplomatic relations.

73

than questionable strategic, requests. For example, upon conclusion of the American involvement in the Vietnam conflict, the United States might agree to turn over to Thailand some fighter aircraft and helicopters, together with limited numbers of technicians. Further assistance in SAMs or other missiles, which Thailand might request for air defense (presumably against Chinese attack), would not seem essential to Thailand's real defense needs and probably should not be granted.

In summary, while reassurance of American support, coupled with continuation and perhaps limited expansion of the assistance program, is likely to forestall major Thai policy shifts, the United States should be prepared to work with an even more self-reliant Thai government. United States interests in Thailand would seem primarily to require that the RTG be assured of a commitment against large-scale invasion. These interests would also appear to dictate resisting Thai efforts to gain sweeping promises from the United States that would allow the RTG to postpone vital internal reforms. The RTG recognizes the numerous differences between its security situation and that in Vietnam and has for some time insisted that it is perfectly capable of handling the insurgency on its own. Within that context, should Bangkok decide to redefine its relationship to the United States, such a move would not seem likely to threaten the basic American interest in preventing domination of that country against the wishes of its leadership and people.

Republic of China. Having contributed some noncombatant training forces and medical teams to the Vietnam war, and having also been sharply critical of America's handling of it, the ROC will certainly want renewed official assurances of America's commitment to its defense in the aftermath of a US withdrawal. Beyond that, the Nationalist government's leverage is limited by dependence on the United States for military assistance and political support; but this would probably not prevent Taipei from seeking to exploit its keen disappointment over US policy by requesting, for instance, a reaffirmation of American defense against Communist attacks on Quemoy and Matsu, a relaxation of restraints on commando raids against the mainland, or increased military assistance to replace outmoded tactical aircraft and to modernize further the oversized army.

As with Thailand, however, the peculiarities of the American relationship with Taiwan pose special problems for the United States commitment. The United States cannot liquidate or ignore its defense obligations under the 1954 treaty without the most profound repercussions on worldwide US commitments and without the risk of signalling to Peking that an invasion of the offshore islands or Taiwan itself could be attempted with impunity. The United States also has what may in the long run be an even more vital interest in working actively toward a moderation of tension with Communist China, an interest in which the role of Taiwan is obviously central. The major question in US-ROC relations consequently is not whether the United States should divorce itself from defense of the island, but how the United States can best stabilize its relations with mainland China while not abandoning Formosa to an uncertain fate.

First, on the matter of the offshore islands of Quemoy and Matsu, the United States would no doubt like to see a Nationalist withdrawal but has been unable to influence a Nationalist decision in that direction. It is clear that the islands add little to the defense of Taiwan against Communist attack (which, if launched, would probably by-pass the heavily fortified islands) and that continued Nationalist control of the islands only increases the chance of a major war crisis in the future. It is equally true that the ROC has significantly improved the living standards of the inhabitants and that Taiwan's population density might make it difficult for the government to absorb willing emigrés. The United States could, of course, threaten to reduce military assistance in proportion to Nationalist expenditures for maintenance of the island garrisons, but it is questionable whether a crisis in relations should be sparked over the offshore islands.

Taiwan remains the major problem. Viewed in terms of a future amelioration of Sino-American tension, the alternative of continuing to support the political claims of the ROC while maintaining present American policy toward the CPR no longer seems tenable. For a more aloof US posture to have meaning, it seems essential that it incorporate important political initiatives toward a Communist Chinese leadership which may be responsive to unexpected American military and diplomatic realignments. The United States might move in either of two directions: Washington might recognize a Republic of Formosa, press for its membership in the United Nations General Assembly, lobby for widespread diplomatic support of the new nation, and in various ways indicate *de facto* recognition of Communist China; or, the United States might maintain political support of the ROC but also extend *de facto* recognition (or its equivalent) to the CPR.

In either case, the United States should consider refraining from converting Taiwan into a major military base, regardless of the future disposition of US bases in Okinawa and the Philippines. The chief Communist claim that the United States "occupies" Taiwan is, of course, groundless, for the Military Advisory Assistance Group (MAAG) now numbers less than 900 men and has been steadily declining in strength. But Peking is on somewhat firmer ground in decrying the use of Taiwan, as during the Vietnam conflict, for American military purposes. It does not seem advisable to augment the ROC's military value to the United States in ways that compromise a future US-CPR détente or a future Formosa-CPR reconciliation. The United States might therefore consider adding to the policy of not assisting any Nationalist recovery plans the policy of not increasing, and in fact continuing to decrease, American military presence on the island.

Both policy alternatives clearly have their respective advantages and disadvantages. Under an independent Formosan republic, the United States would have to be prepared to renounce a long-standing position on the Nationalist claim of representing all the Chinese people *in absentia*. The ultimate step of withdrawing support from the Nationalist leadership would not need to be taken, but the American stance would imply tacit acceptance of the untested but apparently creditable claims of overseas Formosans that the indigenous population aspires to self-determination. An American shift of this order, it should also be noted, would be taking account of a growing dedication among key Nationalist leaders to the development of Taiwan as an independent entity rather than as a springboard for a future recovery operation.[4] Despite this trend, it can be anticipated that if the shift to a one-Taiwan, one-China policy took place with President Chiang still at the helm, Taipei would not hesitate to attack it as a betrayal of trust. The timing of the policy change and the public statements accompanying them might therefore be critical, but the United States would be guided in the direction of change by the overriding purpose of demonstrating to a possibly more moderate Chinese Communist leadership that, while Taiwan will not be cast adrift, the United States is not interested in making Taiwan a military bastion or

[4] See Melvin Gurtov, "Recent Developments on Formosa," *China Quarterly*, no. 31 (July–September 1967), pp. 59–95, for indications of this trend.

in maintaining the fiction of a Chinese government-in-exile.

De facto recognition of two separate Chinese governments has the advantage of changing American policy toward the CPR while sustaining essential elements of the traditional policy toward the ROC. This approach, however, clearly would be as unacceptable to the Nationalist leaders as the first, for in both cases the United States would be rejecting the Nationalists' *raison d'être* in Formosa. Beyond undercutting the legitimacy of Nationalist rule, this second alternative, like the first, would be most unsatisfactory to Taipei and Peking: contrary to the desires of all Chinese, the United States would be trying to promote one or another form of the "two Chinas" solution.

While both approaches seem calculated to prompt an immediately hostile reaction in the two Chinese capitals, on balance the major American interest in working toward a favorable climate of understanding with the CPR would appear best served by focusing on the option of an independent Formosa. Clearly, however, an unfavorable Vietnam settlement, the continuation in power of a Maoist leadership, or a foreign-policy crisis involving Communist China (e.g., over India) would have to be taken into account so far as the timetable and modalities of an American shift on Taiwan are concerned. If, for instance, the United States were to follow a withdrawal from Vietnam under adverse indigenous political circumstances with the immediate announcement of support for an independent Formosan republic, the impact might be to encourage China to take greater risks in the Taiwan Strait rather than to realize the political nature of the American shift. The possibilities for a CPR misreading of American motivations might be lessened if the United States were to introduce hints of a policy shift gradually, with public statements confined to portraying American acknowledgment of the *de facto* control of the China mainland by the

Peking regime.[5] The United States might follow up these statements with quiet diplomatic feelers inside and outside the United Nations to determine the receptivity of Taiwan's supporters to the notion of a separate republic. Finally, the United States might want to delay any irrevocable move toward a Republic of Formosa until the chief antagonists of any form of "two Chinas" solution—Mao Tse-tung and Chiang Kai-shek—have passed from political power.[6] Although there can, of course, be no guarantee that their successors will be more favorably inclined toward a change in the American position, it is hard to visualize two more inflexible regimes than those now in power.

The argument here, in short, favors a two-stage American shift: in the first stage, statements amounting to *de facto* acceptance of the Peking regime amid reassurance of the defense commitment to Taiwan, diplomatic "feelers" to assess the degree of support for an independent Formosa, and continued reduction of the American military presence on Taiwan at least to the pre-Vietnam level; in the second, and assuming a generally favorable response in world capitals to a Formosan republic, selection of the appropriate time for public support of that policy along with public and private reassurances of the American commitment to Taiwan's defense. At that time, if not

[5] An important start in that direction, with appropriate reference to American defense obligations toward Taiwan, was made by Under Secretary of State Nicholas D. Katzenbach in a speech before the National Press Club on May 21, 1968. For the text, see Department of State Publication 8386, East Asian and Pacific Series 175, June 1968.

[6] An alternative approach within the framework of a one-Taiwan, one-China solution should be mentioned. Precisely because mainland China is in upheaval, this approach holds, less radical Communist leaders may be more receptive to an initiative from Washington; Taiwan's image may be enhanced and its chances thereby improved for getting worldwide support now for a separate seat in the General Assembly. The argument therefore runs in favor of attempting a solution to the Taiwan problem before the mainland situation stabilizes.

sooner, it might also be feasible for the United States to begin scaling down military assistance to Formosa, not only to encourage a reconsideration of the practicality of maintaining heavy garrisons on Quemoy and Matsu, but also (and primarily) to limit somewhat the extent to which American assistance could be used by a mainland regime anxious about its political future to suppress the indigenous population.

At the outset, Peking would probably continue to attack any American political moves with respect to Chinese problems as interference. But over the long run, and conceivably though not likely within the next decade, different Chinese leaders might come to recognize that the United States' purpose is to accept their claims to represent a viable and independent China and not to impose a foreign solution on Chinese problems. In fact, the United States might anticipate initial Chinese resentment by proclaiming that recognition of one China and one Formosa does not exclude, and in fact ultimately looks toward, the reconciliation of the island with the mainland, once conditions are appropriate for a free determination on the question of reconciliation by the island's population.

Communist China. While not losing sight of the fact that the United States has legitimate security concerns in Southeast Asia, it is equally important that the United States take positive steps in the interests of regional peace and stability. Deterrent measures hence need to be complemented by other measures which at the least will not further aggravate, and at the most may ameliorate, Sino-American relations. Those measures should not depend on continued caution in the foreign policy of the CPR; rather, they should seek to maximize the choices available to a different Peking leadership willing to give American initiatives a trial hearing. Even if those initiatives should be received at first with indifference or suspicion, as seems likely, they would still have regional and world-wide significance by demonstrating that continued hostile relations are not the product of American intransigence.

The diversified but consistently low-risk nature of CPR foreign policy toward Southeast Asia in recent years, including the period of the Cultural Revolution, would appear to indicate an extremely low likelihood of overt Chinese aggressive behavior in the future, particularly if the Chinese leadership should be dominated by the military. Nevertheless, for the reasons already cited, the United States should maintain in the region a credible capacity to inflict unacceptable damage on any nations which threaten the security of the United States or its allies. Should circumstances compel the United States to reduce or shift its strategic base system in Asia (specifically, Okinawa or the Philippines), it would seem critical that, for the foreseeable future, other facilities be retained (Guam, the Seventh Fleet) and new technological innovations be further developed (advanced Polaris submarines and Poseidon missiles) so that a credible advantage in nuclear and non-nuclear delivery capability is not lost. In this manner, the United States would be able to demonstrate to allied and friendly nations no less than to Peking that a reassessment of American policies toward Asia does not and will not involve a US abandonment of responsibilities there.

With that significant qualification, however, it would seem sensible to accept Chinese competition for the attention and support of its neighbors without fear that Chinese forces or proxy armies will pose a serious threat wherever the United States' commitment is absent. Furthermore, there are several steps the United States might take to promote a more realistic Chinese assessment of American policy and thereby to diminish the prospects of a direct confrontation. The extension of *de facto* recognition to Communist China is one such step. In addition, the United

States might broaden still more the list of categories of persons qualified to travel to mainland China, should Peking accept them. The government might also reconsider the idea, first broached during the Kennedy Administration, of shipping surplus wheat to the CPR in coordination with Australian and Canadian sales. The largely ineffective embargo on trade in nonstrategic commodities could probably be lifted without detriment to the United States inasmuch as trade and investment ties between China and Western Europe are likely to expand anyway. In the United Nations, the United States could support, or at least not oppose, proposals to draw up a compromise formula that would permit Communist China, when ready, to occupy a seat in the General Assembly along with a separate Taiwan delegation. Appropriate UN Charter revisions might also be worked out for the Security Council (perhaps involving an enlarged membership), not necessarily in anticipation of Chinese Communist membership, but in response to the demands of African, Latin American, and Asian members for more proportional representation.

The United States could also go on record as favoring increased direct contacts with Chinese representatives at mutually agreeable sites in Asia. At these or other talks, the United States might indicate a willingness to exchange views on regional arms control and disarmament while leaving open Chinese participation in global or regional arrangements (such as the Nonproliferation Treaty and the Nuclear Test Ban Agreement). Finally, the United States could join with other nations (especially Japan) in inviting active CPR involvement in the Geneva disarmament negotiations, the Asian Development Bank, and the World Bank. All of these proposals have in one way or another been made before; many or all of them might have no immediate interest for Peking. Nevertheless, in forwarding them, the United States would be trying to communicate that it stands ready to discuss any matter of common interest. At the same time, it would have to be expected that CPR reciprocation and concrete achievements toward the realization of a fruitful *modus vivendi* will not be quickly forthcoming and will require infinite patience.

The combination of regional strategic superiority and new diplomatic initiatives toward China does not blithely ignore the possibility of new "wars of national liberation." But the contention is that significant Chinese support of leftist revolutionaries is much less likely to be an attractive alternative for Peking where the United States leaves in indigenous hands the determination of appropriate policies and programs to control them. Communist China is thereby not only given leeway to break away from its substantially self-imposed isolation but is also unchallenged by the American presence in seeking an area-wide détente with its neighbors. The concept supports American containment of (unlikely) Chinese attempts at military expansion, but it also considers that the United States should not seek to (and is really unable to) contain Chinese influence and contacts with other countries.

Policies toward Nonvital Areas of US Interest

The American commitment to seven nations in Asia might be regarded negatively by some as an inescapable, even unfortunate, by-product of extensive historical contact, political interaction, economic relations, and defense treaties. But that commitment also can be viewed as the more durable precisely because it has obligated the United States to defend those Asian nations which have a far greater capacity to help themselves than others in the region. With government bureaucracies generally committed to stability and moderate change, viable political institutions, economies having significant productive potential (and in most cases remarkable growth records), and relatively substantial military resources, these nations seem quite capable of coping on their own with the kinds of threats and pressures to which their enemies are most likely to resort. The bonds between the United States and these allies are consequently stronger because defense responsibilities can be shared; and, as has been suggested, the continuing strength of those bonds in the next decade may depend to a large extent on America's appreciation of the equality of each of its special partners.

For the other nations of Southeast Asia—that is, those in the Indonesian archipelago (Indonesia, Singapore, Malaysia) and mainland Southeast Asia (Burma, Vietnam, Laos, and Cambodia)—native productive, defense, and political capacities have yet to become firmly rooted. These circumstances do not mean that the United States lacks a general interest in assisting them to maintain economic and political stability; what they do imply is that the United States is not and should not become committed to the prevention or reversal of unsatisfactory political trends. At a time when the resources available for the promotion of American interests in Southeast Asia are likely to be very limited, and when political upheaval is likely to remain a major characteristic of the modernizing process in most of Southeast Asia, extreme selectivity would seem to be a particularly appropriate guideline for the involvement of America's prestige and power on behalf of nations that have been defined as secondary interests.

In the case of Laos and Cambodia, the high prospect of military and political pressure from North Vietnam has already been discussed. Since Laos formally dissociated itself from the protection of SEATO in 1962, the American interest there is principally political: to support Laotian neutrality and territorial integrity as stipulated in the

Geneva accords. In Cambodia, the United States has rebuffed the persistent effort of Prince Sihanouk since 1962 to convene an international conference that would provide guarantees for the neutrality and territorial integrity of his country. Close US ties to South Vietnam and Thailand, appreciation of the delicacy of Cambodia's relations with the Vietnam Communists, and several other considerations have also made Washington reluctant to accept the Prince's two preconditions for a restoration of diplomatic relations—namely, recognition of and respect for Cambodia's present borders. Yet, despite these and other policy differences, Cambodia and the United States share suspicions about Vietnamese Communist intentions in Indochina, recognize the importance of Cambodian neutralism and the international respect it has gained, and acknowledge the indirect contributions an American military presence in Southeast Asia makes to Cambodia's security.

In light of these circumstances, American energies might best be utilized in Laos to convene another international conference as one step toward moving the confrontation there from the battlefield to the bargaining table. The United States would thereby acknowledge the present *de facto* territorial division in Laos and the futility of supporting further military efforts to achieve a non-communist Laos. But for the United States to attract North Vietnamese, as well as Soviet and Chinese, interest in such a conference, Washington would have to make it clear that the conference's purpose would not be limited to renewing promises of respect for Laotian territorial integrity but would also seek to encourage a political settlement arrived at by the competing Laotian factions. North Vietnam could then expect the Pathet Lao to obtain political representation in Vientiane commensurate with their military power. Hanoi might further consider that with control of the neighboring Laotian provinces of Sam Neua and Phong Saly in friendly hands, its security interests would be satisfied.

In Cambodia, as in Laos, American influence may more effectively be brought to bear through a combination of diplomatic initiatives and a military presence outside Indochina than through new commitments. Sihanouk believes that he cannot expect any real security guarantees from the major powers, now including Communist China, or any meaningful protection by the International Control Commission (ICC) against border incursions. His convictions largely explain Cambodia's outwardly friendly and accommodating attitude toward the Vietnamese Communists, based on the hope that they will abide by their promises (made in mid-1967) to respect Cambodia's borders. Nevertheless, Sihanouk might welcome a new Geneva conference to reaffirm respect for his country's frontiers, neutrality, and territorial integrity even without guarantees, which would probably be ineffective and, from the US standpoint, undesirable. Unlike a decision to strengthen the ICC, a new international conference would focus world attention on Cambodia's borders possibly without aggravating Cambodian-Vietnamese Communist relations. So long as Cambodia defers to Hanoi, in particular through political support and a vocal anti-imperialist international stance, Hanoi's interests are probably satisfied. At the same time, the fact that the United States would not be operating economic or military aid programs in Cambodia would give Sihanouk some leverage: it would allow him to combat Communist pressure by threatening to resume aid ties with the United States.

Within the context of diplomatic options, the United States might also seek to take advantage of any disposition on the part of North Vietnam to widen its contacts with the non-Communist world. As effective as Hanoi has been in exploiting the Sino-Soviet rift to acquire war materiel, agricultural commodities, and aid in the development of light and heavy industry, its leaders are undoubtedly aware of the nation's dependence on Moscow and Peking—a dependence that will increase during the period of postwar recovery. It may therefore be worthwhile for the United States to test again the DRV's receptivity to becoming involved in such regional economic undertakings as the Mekong Development Project or the Asian Development Bank, membership in which would qualify Hanoi for financial aid. In view of certain congressional opposition to any form of aid to "the enemy," the next administration might want to hinge Hanoi's participation in regional projects, or even American assistance to a multi-nation, perhaps UN-administered Vietnam relief and rehabilitation fund, on Hanoi's good faith in abiding by the 1962 agreements on Laos.

Admittedly, the North Vietnamese may well reject another conference on Laos or Cambodia and rebuff American "feelers" of aid—in short, pursue their ambitions in Indochina under the same low-risk, low-cost strategy they have followed in recent years. Should this latter situation obtain, the United States could do little to prevent Laos and Cambodia from falling within Hanoi's sphere of influence, short of embarking on a massive commitment of men and resources that would seem from many standpoints highly infeasible and undesirable.

Elsewhere in the region, the dangers to political stability seem to stem mainly from within individual countries rather than from outside. In Burma and Indonesia, for instance, the Communist parties are plagued by traditional factionalism, ineffective leadership, and military defeats (in the former case), and by severe government repression in the wake of an abortive coup attempt (in the latter). Despite Communist China's support (predominantly verbal) of the CPB-White Flags and the shattered Communist Party of Indonesia (PKI), the prospects for both parties will depend primarily on the dedication shown by the central governments toward solving old problems of a nonideological nature. Where government attention to the Communist threat absorbs more resources than programs of national reconciliation aimed at disaffected ethnic and religious minorities, national integration is bound to become an even more distant goal.

Singapore and Malaysia share with Indonesia the difficulties of dealing with heterogenous populations whose potential for racial conflict is well known. The Barisan Socialists in Singapore and the Chinese rebel leader Chin Peng's Liberation Army in Malaya have consistently sought to exploit racial tensions but with little impact thus far on the stability of the central governments. In this particular region, furthermore, there are major unsettled political and territorial disputes which will contribute to anxieties over subregional security after the British withdrawal in 1971. Malaysian-Filipino tension over Sabah is only the latest manifestation of continued intra-regional strife. Insofar as the *external* Communist threat is concerned, however, Singapore, Malaysia, and Indonesia are favored by their geographical position: unlike Burma, Laos, and Cambodia, their distance from North Vietnam and China makes any future insurgent threat significantly easier to handle.[7] Although it is still too early to tell, the announcement of the British withdrawal, together with events in Vietnam, may eventually push these three states (along with Australia and New Zealand) into joining more closely together—in defense and trade, for instance—to pro-

---

[7] The Malaysian government's main problem with a Communist sanctuary is along the border with southern Thailand, where Chin Peng's roughly 500- to 800-man force operates. But Thai-Malaysian border cooperation is also more extensive than anywhere else in Southeast Asia. Despite an increase in Communist-initiated violence during 1968 in the border region, the bilateral agreements concluded on border patrolling and limited pursuit across the frontier promise to keep Communist armed action at a low level.

mote national self-help within the framework of subregional collaboration.

This overview of Burma, Indonesia, Singapore, and Malaysia may be sufficient to permit at least some observations about the implications of their security and security-related problems for US policy. In these four countries, insurgency or political violence has been part of a long-term process of political development and social modernization. The meaning of this process for the United States would seem to be that very little influence can be brought to bear on its outcome. Upsets of the *status quo* are likely to be normal features of political development in those countries for some time to come, and the United States might not always find itself out of sympathy with revolutionary movements. In contrast to the countries specified as vital interests of the United States, moreover, these four nations, like Laos and Cambodia, have not yet passed through the period of political tutelage, have long histories of involvement with colonial powers, and as yet seem unable (for widely different reasons) to deal with externally-supported security threats on their own. These factors compound the dilemmas that would be posed for the United States in considering any new commitments—commitments, it should be added, which are by no means uniformly desired. Clearly the events of September–October 1965 in Indonesia, the ability of Burma to preserve its neutralism in the face of China's Cultural Revolution, and the encouraging record of economic progress in Malaysia and Singapore underscore the proposition being advanced here that the general American interest in stability and development in Southeast Asia can be promoted not only in the absence of direct commitments but also with some confidence in the capacities of these nations to preserve their independence even as they undergo occasionally volatile internal change.

The United States may therefore continue to find

greater long-term value in stimulating an environment of mutual interaction among these Asian states—by contributing to, but not directing, regional economic and cultural cooperation, and by refraining from pressuring the nations in the area to commit themselves to particular alliances, policies, or ideologies—than in vigorously exercising American power and influence on behalf of particular regimes. American military support may sometimes be useful, but in general, the United States would seem more capable of influencing developments in Southeast Asia through well-administered economic assistance programs, to the extent possible on a multilateral basis. By attempting to enhance the economic and political stability of interested Southeast Asian nations in this way, the security environment may be strengthened over the long run as nations in the region are further encouraged to concentrate on internal problems and to seek solutions in regional economic collaboration and major-power aid. Conceivably, of course, their determined attack on internal causes of social unrest, cultural prejudices, and economic inequalities could create a climate of whirlwind change in which unfriendly revolutionary movements might thrive. But such an attack, encouraged and assisted by the United States, would be far more likely to lead to less dangerous, less frequent social instability that would in turn fortify native political institutions.

American Assistance Programs. Whether for vital allies or for other nations in Southeast Asia, the United States will almost certainly have limited aid funds to dispense after withdrawing from Vietnam and perhaps for years to come. Further, the administration will probably have greater difficulty in justifying assistance to Southeast Asia, especially military assistance administered on a bilateral basis. The guidelines below are therefore proposed with an awareness of the probable political constraints on foreign-aid spending. While the emphasis is as much on multilateral as on bilateral programs, any administration will, at least initially, probably have to muster all its political weapons to gain support for multilateral programs and will in any case be restricted in contributions to nations of secondary interest by the demands of major allies (notably Thailand and South Korea). If there is any compensation in all of this, it may be that administration backing of subregional economic cooperation, by putting the stress on Asian self-help, may not only help remove the political onus from foreign aid but may also be more appealing to Congress and the public if proposed as a means of stretching the aid dollar's value.

Among the available multilateral agencies, consideration might be given to working for an expansion of the role of the Economic Commission on Asia and the Far East (ECAFE) under the Economic and Social Council. Since ECAFE is funded through the regular UN budget, a larger share of AID dollars might be offered to enlarge the budget and simultaneously to allay the suspicions of other nations, notably the Soviet Union, toward fuller American participation in international lending institutions. ECAFE might be persuaded to become involved in additional multilateral programs in Southeast Asia—like the Mekong River Valley project—in cooperation with the Asian Development Bank (ADB) and other organizations. By encouraging ECAFE to organize specific sectoral rather than overambitious regional undertakings, and also by inviting the participation of the Vietnamese government(s), the United States would be clearly manifesting the genuineness of its interest in furthering economic development in Southeast Asia strictly on the bases of economic feasibility and predictable benefit to the nations concerned.

Cooperation between ECAFE and such institutions as the ADB on specific pilot projects is based on the belief that the time is not yet ripe for attempting or supporting region-wide economic endeavors. The full-fledged economic integration of Southeast Asia implied by such endeavors is still a very distant goal because of the political hostilities among the nations of the region and because of their different levels of economic growth and attainment. If sectoral projects for the removal of trade barriers, the development of irrigation and electrification, or the establishment of a common steel plant, can prove their economic worth and feasibility, there may arise a common recognition of the advantages of still broader undertakings to achieve economies of scale in industry and to avoid duplication of effort, as in agricultural exports. Even then, however, the barriers to sectoral integration are imposing, and progress toward it is bound to be halting during the next decade.

Bilaterally, American economic assistance might meet with more widespread Asian approval if more of it were offered through the Colombo Plan. Under the auspices of the Plan, which provides a meeting ground for Asian and Western nations through regular conferences, bilateral capital and technical assistance agreements have been concluded for specific projects. The Colombo Plan has earned a reputation for respectability; only in a few isolated instances have aid recipients complained about political pressure by donor nations. For the United States, the advantages of working through the Colombo Plan are that the organization is Asian-run, that aid can be geared to specific projects whose progress could be followed outside the framework of AID missions in the recipient countries, and that the government will probably run a smaller risk of being accused of political interference. Finally, since such countries as Burma and Cambodia are Colombo Plan members but do not belong to Asian organizations like ASEAN and ASPAC, the Plan might come to provide a source for these two countries to obtain American support without having to compromise their neutralism. Moreover, America's extension of aid to these countries would answer the criticism that only pro-Western governments and alliances can expect dollar grants.

Aside from working through multilateral and bilateral agencies, the United States might give thought to excluding Southeast Asia from the general practice of tying assistance to the purchase of American goods. While such conditional aid is important in the West European context, it may impose an undue hardship on the Southeast Asian nations out of proportion to the benefits to the US balance of payments. The United States might also encourage an expanded program of technical exchange through specialized Asian and American aid teams. Taiwan and Japan, for instance, have scored impressive achievements in their respective programs of agricultural and technical assistance projects to Southeast Asia and Africa. Futher exchanges within the Asia region, with each nation dispatching experts in agriculture and industry to meet the specific requirements of neighboring countries, could result in handsome returns quite beyond mere economics. In this area, the United States might consider sending its own teams (e.g., sanitation and health specialists) and underwriting or encouraging ADB underwriting of other exchanges by nations unable to support them.

Parallel with these multilateral undertakings, the United States might want to expand cost-sharing arrangements with the Soviet Union and Japan. If Moscow substantially increases its economic stakes in Southeast Asia during the coming ten years, it would clearly be in American interests to have collaborative, though probably of necessity independent, assistance efforts in Asia play some part in the search for new avenues of détente. In practice, the Soviet Union is already engaged in competitive cooperation with the United States and other countries in the large-scale assistance program to India. Moscow might continue to be encouraged, moreover, to become more active in ECAFE and to join the ADB. Recent Soviet comments on regional cooperation in Southeast Asia draw an interesting distinction between such organizations as ASA, ASPAC, and ASEAN, which are considered instruments of the American security program, and an international organization like ECAFE, which is highly praised for providing practical assistance and is more accessible to Soviet influence.[8]

Active bilateral trade relationships between the USSR and the Asian countries—including Thailand, Malaysia, Singapore, and the Philippines—may be potentially beneficial to economic development by broadening these nations' economic contacts and thereby demonstrating the value of extra-regional trade.[9] In Thailand's case, enlarged contacts with Moscow might also provide a useful lever against DRV ambitions in Laos, since Hanoi will probably have to rely on Soviet help for postwar reconstruction. At a time when the United States would be concentrating assistance on the nonmilitary side, the Soviet Union might eventually be persuaded that its influence in Southeast Asia could be extended more cheaply than before—by involvement in the region's economic activities instead of primarily through major military assistance programs in support of undependable, ideologically variegated bourgeois socialist or bureaucratic military regimes. There is, of course, no guarantee that the Soviets

[8] "Regional Co-operation in South-East Asia: Soviet Misgivings," *Mizan*, vol. IX, no. 6 (November–December 1967), pp. 252–57.

[9] As Charles Wolf, Jr., has pointed out, the different economic interests and development levels of countries such as these, no less than those of Japan, would seem to call for some qualification of a strictly regional or subregional approach to economic development. For some purposes, economic associations with Europe and the Americas might be far more fruitful. See *Japan-U.S. Relations and Asian Development Problems* (Santa Monica, Calif.: The RAND Corporation, Paper P-3825, April 1968).

94

will react in this way, but if they seek to replace US military aid with their own—perhaps to gain leverage for demanding base rights (as in India)—they are very likely to find considerable opposition in Southeast Asia to this kind of aid blackmail.

Japanese involvement in the economic activities of Southeast Asia suggests different problems, some of which have already been enumerated. Inasmuch as Japan has already revealed great conservatism in its approach to investment and assistance there, no Japanese government is likely to take on a leading role in underwriting Southeast Asian development programs in the future in order to ease American responsibilities. American encouragement of the Japanese to become further participants in regional development would probably have to be coupled to a clear demonstration of a continuing US financial commitment. Here again, of course, limited American resources may indicate precisely the opposite not only to Japan but also to other nations that have placed their hopes on regionalism in one or another form.

Within its limitations, however, the United States might substantially increase its financial contributions to multilateral arrangements as a means of encouraging the Japanese, by the American example, to make greater use of multilateral agencies for the dispensation of technical and other assistance. Japan's preparedness to undertake a larger share probably will continue to depend on whether certain projects have profit potential. Tokyo will doubtless insist, for example, on tying Japanese aid to purchases of Japanese goods. Beyond this, and short of direct American economic pressure, there seems little the United States can do to obtain substantial Japanese aid and overseas investment of an order that might help defray American costs.

With Japan, as with the rest of Southeast Asia, then, the next decade stands as a trying one for the promotion of economic growth. How external assistance toward the promotion of independent national development can be provided without imposing on the United States the political stigma of direct management, without appearing to compromise the image of Asian "self-help" which the region's nations increasingly value, and without committing the United States to a financial burden that is unrealistically large, given other priorities, is almost certain to become an increasingly acute problem with increasingly unsatisfactory answers.

Regionalism: The Military Side. Parallel with the growth of economically oriented regional and subregional organizations, many of the nations there may become seriously interested in new kinds of military alignments. As yet, the Asian nations aligned with or friendly to the United States have failed to reach agreement on the ramifications of new military ties. The Malaysians have suggested expanding ASEAN into the security field. Thailand, though apparently determined to play a leading role in regional economic cooperation and the resolution of regional disputes (as, for example, in the Malaysia-Philippines controversy over Sabah), has shied away from the security alternative, even though Bangkok has long considered the SEATO pact weak and ineffectual. In anticipation of the British withdrawal from Singapore, Malaysia and Singapore have reached a preliminary agreement to combine air defenses; and Australia, New Zealand, Malaysia, and Singapore evidently hope to maintain Singapore as a central naval installation, though leaving it unclear whose military vessels are supposed to be operating from there.

While these proposals and developments, if representative of a genuine trend, may seem to have positive implications for US security objectives in the Southeast Asia of the near future, they contain a number of negative features. On the surface, any coalescing of non-Communist nations would appear to promote precisely the kind of self-help and regional security interdependence which American policy has been striving to achieve for nearly twenty years. But, in the first place, appeals for regional military unity have been based on China's believed capacity to promote and sustain wars of national liberation. The formation of new anti-Communist alliances is one of the surest ways to attract at least verbal Chinese support of revolutionary movements in the participating countries. (It is also likely to discourage any future serious Soviet interest in working with regional economic groups.)

Second, rationalization of new alliances in terms of the China threat may lead to a diversion of fiscal (including American aid) and industrial resources into defense production, and may prompt calls upon the United States to provide the tactical aircraft, technical support, and related equipment needed to ensure the implementation of self-help. Third, military collaboration would seem to be a primary example of misplaced emphasis if it does not evolve out of progress in independent economic and political development. Thailand's reluctance to become committed to militarizing ASEAN or ASPAC has made it clear that nations should first devote themselves to eradicating conditions that permit revolutionary movements to prosper rather than collaborate to identify and liquidate insurgents. Finally, new organizations geared to suppressing internal subversion might entangle the United States in opposing revolutionist acts or movements (left or right) having aims which might be favorable to American interests.

This negative side to the coin of military regionalism seems to point to the need for the United States to examine carefully the scope of any new Asian military arrangements and the extent to which the United States could support them. Certain types of military collaborations, such as nonaggression pacts and bi-nation agreements on border surveillance (e.g., Thailand-Malaysia or Thailand-Laos), would not seem to present any obstacle to US support.

These agreements, after all, are geared to the particular goal of enhancing security through assurances regarding national frontiers. Unlike military pacts, such cooperative arrangements do not require American military assistance or political commitments. An important consequence is that the United States cannot compromise these efforts by leaving them open to being branded as American-led anti-Communist alliances. Nor would the United States become committed to backing specific (and perhaps undesirable) regimes eager for major-power approval, especially in times of domestic upheaval.

Realistically speaking, the United States will probably find it difficult to reject petitions for support of other forms of military cooperation in Southeast Asia, however questionable their usefulness in terms of the real security problems in the region. The difficulty rests, of course, in the fact of long-standing American support for Asian initiatives on defense matters; it may also arise if key American allies (Thailand and the Philippines) become participants. Yet the United States should still be able to place appropriate limitations on the extent of its support.

Should new military organizations involving American allies be formed, the United States might stress that such assistance as will be given should be subject to certain conditions. The first might be that bilateral US military aid will probably have to be diminished in rough proportion to aid earmarked for the use of multilateral defense associations; second, that US aid shall not be used (as it has been in Thailand) for strengthening the control of the government in power rather than to promote security from external aggression or internal, alien-oriented subversion. Above all, the United States should not make promises of air and naval assistance, whether involving US military personnel or not, to bolster countersubversion Asian military arrangements. As has long been the case throughout the history of the American involvement in Vietnam, and more recently in Thailand, such promises raise political problems and create friction instead of resolving alleged and real security threats.

The establishment of a new all-Asian security organization, perhaps taking on the shape and tasks of SEATO, would neither assure its military effectiveness nor preclude SEATO from continuing to serve a useful purpose. It is perfectly true that SEATO's usefulness has been sharply undercut in recent years by the *de facto* withdrawals of France and Pakistan (and, in 1971, Great Britain as well) and that the organization merely duplicates existing bilateral defense commitments of the United States. Nevertheless, SEATO retains a certain psychological value by indicating an American interest in Southeast Asia's security problems in a public but limited fashion. That value will be especially important after an American withdrawal from Vietnam. In fact, the United States may want to give serious consideration at that time, when tangible evidence of a continuing American interest in Southeast Asian security is demanded by allies, to using the SEATO framework for the purpose of periodically conducting show-the-flag military exercises in the South China Sea or the western Pacific. By demonstrating a capacity to deploy ground forces to the theater quickly from the continental United States or air and naval (including Polaris/ Poseidon) forces from overseas bases, the United States could underscore its mobility in responding to crises, its continued concern over the whole range of possible war situations, and its sustained interest in backing allied nations through the medium of SEATO. Reiterative displays of this kind might also serve as the American alternative to invitations from allied and/or friendly nations for direct American association with other multilateral security ventures. They might also considerably reduce the anxieties already expressed by many of those nations that neither the Nonproliferation Treaty nor the Tri-Nation Security Council resolution provides dependable guarantees of protection against the (Chinese) threat of nuclear attack.

VI

CONCLUSION

The theme of this study has been that, given an eventual American withdrawal from Vietnam, the time is propitious for a complete reassessment of American roles and responsibilities in Southeast Asia. By more specifically defining the scope and nature of American concern, new ways may be found to preserve the national interest while accepting the inevitable inconveniences to the national influence. A reduction of US involvement in Southeast Asia, without retracting existing security commitments, is the major alternative proposed. The contrary view holds that any restructuring of American policies and programs would carry unacceptably high risks to the national interest. Further, this view maintains that the non-Communist nations of Southeast Asia may, despite American reassurances and compensatory measures, be drawn into an intensive reappraisal of their interests. Some of them may attempt various kinds of compromises with local Communist organizations or major Communist powers, thereby strengthening the Communist position in the region. Thus, however desirable less involvement in Southeast Asia may be in the abstract, the United States simply cannot afford to make significant departures from present policy without possibly undermining the whole structure of regional security.

To begin with, this study has maintained that the United States has no vital security interests in Southeast Asia; the takeover of any single country there by forces hostile to the United States would not seriously threaten the security of the United States. While the United States does have a broad security function to perform—namely, preventing any one hostile power from dominating the region as a whole—and does have certain nonsecurity interests requiring the protection of specific countries from aggression, the challenging question for the United States in coming years will not be how to respond to overt aggression but how to understand and deal with the implications of dynamic change and political confusion for regional stability. Insofar as this latter problem is concerned, it is asserted here that at the stage of political and social transition in which all the nations of the Southeast Asian region now find themselves, the United States simply cannot expect to do more than marginally influence the establishment of a lasting, set pattern of stability conducive to the eventual evolution of non-Communist, pluralistic societies. To argue otherwise is to support the dubious assumption that present political affinities in the region accurately reflect deeply held, permanent ideological convictions connoting a sharing of values with American (or any other) tenets and ideals. Nationalism, as the most powerful and most prevalent force in Southeast Asia, can be appreciated and reckoned with, but it is not an ideology that arises out of philosophical persuasion. Whether nationalism expresses itself in a neutral, leftist, or rightist direction is therefore far more likely to be a consequence of the interplay of indigenous and big-power politics than of a genuine adherence by individual regimes to one or another foreign doctrine.

As has been suggested, moreover, it is extremely doubtful that Southeast Asian nations will in wholesale fashion accommodate to local or external Communist forces so long as the United States makes clear by word and deed that withdrawal from Vietnam does not mean outright withdrawal from Asia. But should certain of those nations (as is already the case to some extent) begin to reconsider which policies are in their own best interests and then to adapt accordingly, this reconsideration would not be at all inconsistent with the unsettled quality of regional politics just mentioned; nor would American interests necessarily be adversely affected. On the contrary, it would reaffirm that practical considerations rather than doctrinal loyalties are these nations' principal guides to action. Should some of them go so far as to be replaced by elements unfriendly to the United States, the extreme thinness of the fabric of those governments would be starkly revealed. For if some governments should prove unable or unwilling to handle internally generated security threats—despite evidence that the United States has no intention of abandoning its primary responsibilities in the region—then increased assistance, or, in the extreme, the direct backing of American military power would hardly seem to be either a feasible or desirable alternative.

Those who object that Communist forces will probably gain from uncertainty over the United States' future security role in the region would seem to exaggerate the dimensions of the threat posed and the capabilities of the United States to influence developments there. The objection further betrays an oversimplification of the nature of the threat and an overestimation of the depth of the American commitment to oppose it. Revolutionary leftism is, after all, not the only undesirable trend in Southeast Asia. The inherent instability in the region may also provide the occasion for the rise of, or strengthening of, anti-Communist right-wing regimes pursuing fascist policies which the United States might not wish to support. Economic development and political progress in Southeast Asia can be (and has been) hampered as much by rightist as by

103

leftist regimes; and de-stabilizing internal threats can as often stem from the progressive right as from the left. In the future, the United States may find itself in sympathy with elements committed to leftist programs. In these circumstances, it would seem highly questionable for the United States to adhere to any single standard in determining a response to political oppositions or revolutionary movements, particularly as hostility to the *status quo* may sometimes be desirable from the standpoint of American interests.

The need for flexibility in dealing with revolutionary situations in Southeast Asia applies equally to allies of the United States. The United States has made commitments to the security of particular nations from external domination, not to the preservation of reprehensible governments. A vital American interest in protecting a nation against external aggression needs to be distinguished, in other words, from overidentification with particular regimes whose ineffectiveness or unsavory governmental processes run against the grain of American values. Of course, the United States should not, and probably never could, impose its values on another political system; but neither need the United States act so as to create or give the impression of having a vested interest in the continuation in power of regimes carrying out undesirable political, social, or economic policies. This is an admittedly difficult guideline to follow in practice. But in adopting an aloof posture toward Southeast Asia—by which is meant upholding existing commitments while making clear their limitations and enlarging the avenues for adaptations and modifications of existing national relations—the United States may indirectly be able to influence more positive contributions by allies to political equality without fear that they will collapse or that Communist forces will be able to breach their security. In fact, by initiating modifications of its own (toward Communist China), the United States may ultimately enhance the security prospects of these and other nations in Southeast Asia.

There are consequently no grounds for assuming the worst in Southeast Asia immediately after the United States withdraws from Vietnam, nor once the United States adopts a new policy course toward the region. In both cases the consequences of American initiatives will be ambiguous, for such is the nature of politics and foreign policy there. The American attitude toward the region may therefore come to be as important as American policies. If the United States demonstrates its confidence in the ability of the region's governments to determine their own destinies and gives evidence of a flexible approach toward allies and major hostile powers, Southeast Asia may move more rapidly toward the stability that has evaded it since the colonial era.

SELECTED RAND BOOKS

Brodie, Bernard. *STRATEGY IN THE MISSILE AGE.* Princeton, N.J.: Princeton University Press, 1959.

Davison, W. Phillips. *THE BERLIN BLOCKADE: A STUDY IN COLD WAR POLITICS.* Princeton, N.J.: Princeton University Press, 1958.

Dinerstein, H. S. and Leon Gouré. *TWO STUDIES IN SOVIET CONTROLS: COMMUNISM AND THE RUSSIAN PEASANT; MOSCOW IN CRISIS.* Glencoe, Ill.: The Free Press, 1955.

Dinerstein, H. S. *WAR AND THE SOVIET UNION: NUCLEAR WEAPONS AND THE REVOLUTION IN SOVIET MILITARY AND POLITICAL THINKING.* New York: Frederick A. Praeger, 1959.

Garthoff, Raymond L. *SOVIET MILITARY DOCTRINE.* Glencoe, Ill.: The Free Press, 1953.

George, Alexander L. *PROPAGANDA ANALYSIS: A STUDY OF INFERENCES MADE FROM NAZI PROPAGANDA IN WORLD WAR II.* Evanston, Ill.: Row, Peterson and Company, 1959.

Gouré, Leon. *CIVIL DEFENSE IN THE SOVIET UNION.* Los Angeles, Calif.: University of California Press, 1962.

Gouré, Leon. *THE SIEGE OF LENINGRAD.* Stanford, Calif.: Stanford University Press, 1962.

Halpern, Manfred. *THE POLITICS OF SOCIAL CHANGE IN THE MIDDLE EAST AND NORTH AFRICA.* Princeton, N.J.: Princeton University Press, 1963.

Hitch, Charles J. and Roland McKean. *THE ECONOMICS OF DEFENSE IN THE NUCLEAR AGE.* Cambridge, Mass.: Harvard University Press, 1960.

Horelick, Arnold L. and Myron Rush. *STRATEGIC POWER AND SOVIET FOREIGN POLICY.* Chicago, Ill.: University of Chicago Press, 1966.

Hsieh, Alice Langley. *COMMUNIST CHINA'S STRATEGY IN THE NUCLEAR ERA.* Englewood Cliffs, N.J.: Prentice-Hall, 1962.

Johnson, John J. (ed.). *THE ROLE OF THE MILITARY IN UNDERDEVELOPED COUNTRIES.* Princeton, N.J.: Princeton University Press, 1962.

Johnstone, William C. *BURMA'S FOREIGN POLICY: A STUDY IN NEUTRALISM.* Cambridge, Mass.: Harvard University Press, 1963.

Kecskemeti, Paul. *THE UNEXPECTED REVOLUTION.* Stanford, Calif.: Stanford University Press, 1961.

Kolkowicz, Roman. *THE SOVIET MILITARY AND THE COMMUNIST PARTY.* Princeton, N.J.: Princeton University Press, 1967.

Leites, Nathan. *A STUDY OF BOLSHEVISM.* Glencoe, Ill.: The Free Press, 1953.

Leites, Nathan. *ON THE GAME OF POLITICS IN FRANCE.* Stanford, Calif.: Stanford University Press, 1959.

Leites, Nathan. *THE OPERATIONAL CODE OF THE POLITBURO.* New York: McGraw-Hill Book Company, 1951.

Liu, Ta-Chung and Kung-Chia Yeh. *THE ECONOMY OF THE CHINESE MAINLAND: NATIONAL INCOME AND ECONOMIC DEVELOPMENT, 1933–1959.* Princeton, N.J.: Princeton University Press, 1965.

108

Melnik, Constantin and Nathan Leites. *THE HOUSE WITH-OUT WINDOWS: FRANCE SELECTS A PRESIDENT.* Evanston, Ill.: Row, Peterson and Company, 1958.

Quade, E. S. (ed.). *ANALYSIS FOR MILITARY DECISIONS.* Chicago, Ill.: Rand McNally & Company; Amsterdam, Netherlands: North-Holland Publishing Company, 1964.

Quade, E. S. and W. I. Boucher. *SYSTEMS ANALYSIS AND POLICY PLANNING APPLICATION IN DEFENSE.* New York: American Elsevier Pub. Co., 1968.

Rosen, George. *DEMOCRACY AND ECONOMIC CHANGE IN INDIA.* Berkeley and Los Angeles, Calif.: University of California Press, 1966.

Rush, Myron. *POLITICAL SUCCESSION IN THE USSR.* New York: Columbia University Press, 1965.

Rush, Myron. *THE RISE OF KHRUSHCHEV.* Washington, D.C.: Public Affairs Press, 1958.

Scalapino, Robert A. *THE JAPANESE COMMUNIST MOVEMENT, 1920–1966.* Berkeley and Los Angeles, Calif.: University of California Press, 1967.

Selznick, Philip. *THE ORGANIZATIONAL WEAPON: A STUDY OF BOLSHEVIK STRATEGY AND TACTICS.* New York: McGraw-Hill Book Company, 1952.

Sokolovskii, V. D. (ed.). *SOVIET MILITARY STRATEGY.* Englewood Cliffs, N.J.: Prentice-Hall, 1963.

Speier, Hans. *DIVIDED BERLIN: THE ANATOMY OF SOVIET POLITICAL BLACKMAIL.* New York: Frederick A. Praeger, 1961.

Speier, Hans. *GERMAN REARMAMENT AND ATOMIC WAR: THE VIEWS OF GERMAN MILITARY AND POLITICAL LEADERS.* Evanston, Ill.: Row, Peterson, and Company, 1957.

Speier, Hans and W. Phillips Davison (eds.). *WEST GERMAN LEADERSHIP AND FOREIGN POLICY.* Evanston, Ill.: Row, Peterson and Company, 1957.

Tanham, G. K. *COMMUNIST REVOLUTIONARY WAR-FARE: THE VIETMINH IN INDOCHINA*. New York: Frederick A. Praeger, 1961.

Trager, Frank N. (ed.). *MARXISM IN SOUTHEAST ASIA: A STUDY OF FOUR COUNTRIES*. Stanford, Calif.: Stanford University Press, 1959.

Whiting, Allen S. *CHINA CROSSES THE YALU: THE DECISION TO ENTER THE KOREAN WAR*. New York: The Macmillan Company, 1960.

Wolf, Charles Jr. *FOREIGN AID: THEORY AND PRAC-TICE IN SOUTHERN ASIA*. Princeton, N.J.: Princeton University Press, 1960.

Wolfe, Thomas W. *SOVIET STRATEGY AT THE CROSS-ROADS*. Cambridge, Mass.: Harvard University Press, 1964.

INDEX

Afro-Asian Conference (Bandung), 3
Anti-ballistic missile (ABM) system, 66
Arab Israeli war (June 1967), 58
Asia and Pacific Council, the (ASPAC), 62, 92, 94, 97
Asian Development Bank (ADB), 61, 82, 87, 91, 93, 94
Association of South-East Asian Nations (ASEAN), 42, 43, 72, 92, 94, 96, 97
Australia, 11, 32, 35, 82
  and British withdrawal from Singapore, 42–43
  Japanese relations with, 60
  US interests in, 36–37
  US policies toward, 64–67, 96
Australia – New Zealand – United States (ANZUS) Treaty, 37, 64, 65

Balance of power, 9, 32
Barisan Socialists, see Singapore
Brezhnev, Leonid, 58
Bull, Hedley, 11, 65, 66
Burma, 20, 39, 43, 44
  Chinese policy toward, 15–16, 22–24, 26–29
  and the Colombo Plan, 92
  future US policies toward, 84, 87, 88
  Soviet relations with, 55, 59

Cambodia, 16, 17, 22, 23, 27, 39, 44
  China's interest in, 26

Communist pressure on, 71
  and the Colombo Plan, 92
  future US policies toward, 84–89
  Soviet relations with, 55, 59
Canberra talks of June 1969, 67
Ceylon, 23, 27
Chiang Kai-shek, 77, 79
Chinese Communist Party (CCP), 49, 55
Chinese People's Republic (CPR), 15, 20, 21, 25, 26, 27, 28, 38, 48ff., 56, 76, 78, 80–83
  armed forces of the, 51
  as a nuclear power, 45, 55–57, 65
  and assistance to Viet Minh, 3
  and the "Cultural Revolution," 4, 22, 23, 26, 48, 49, 54, 58, 81, 89
  domestic uncertainty in the, 48–50
  erosion of reputation of the, 23, 26
  foreign policy of the, 51, 52
  future US policies toward the, 80–83
  primary goals of the, 26
  relations of the, with the USSR, 4, 53–55, 58, 86
  relations of the, with the US, 52, 77, 80, 81
  relations of the, with Southeast Asia, 22, 41
Chin Peng, 88
Chou En-lai, 48
Colombo Plan, 92

111

Comintern Southeast Asia Bureau, 16
Communist party
  of Burma (CPB), 15, 26–28, 73, 86
  of Indonesia (PKI), 87
  of Thailand (CPT), 25, 73
Containment strategy, 4

Democratic Republic of Vietnam (DRV), 13, 17, 18, 25, 85, 86, 87, 94
  Peking opposition to, 18
Domino principle, 2, 4, 9, 13

Economic Commission on Asia and the Far East (ECAFE), 91
Eisenhower Administration, 1, 2

Fortress America, 9
Fortress Australia, 65

Geneva Conference
  1954, 2, 16
  1961–62, 70
  on Cambodia, 86
Great Britain, see Singapore, British withdrawal from
Greene, Fred, 32–34

Ho Chi Minh, 16, 18

India, 20, 33, 93
  China's policy toward, 28–29
Indochina, 1, 2
Indochinese Communist Party (ICP), 16
Indonesia, 11, 20, 39
  economic development of, 45
  future US policies toward, 39, 84, 87, 88, 89
  Japanese economic interests in, 6
  and regionalism, 44
Insurgency, 7, 15, 29, 89
  in Thailand, 71, 73
  as people's war, 20, 21, 24
  effect of Vietnam on, 14
International Control Commission (ICC), 86

Japan, 11, 32, 35

future US policies toward, 93, 95, 96
  in Southeast Asia, 41, 60–62
  Soviet relations with, 59–60
  value of, to US, 35–36, 40
Johnson, Lyndon B., 9

Katzenbach, Nicholas D., 79n
Kecskemeti, Paul, 20, 21
Kennedy Administration, 82
Khmer Viet Minh, 17, 18
Kuala Lumpur (Conference of 1968), 11

Lao Dong (Workers') Party, 20
Laos, 16, 17, 20, 24, 39, 47
  China's interest in, 26
  Communist takeover of, 71
  future US policy toward, 84–89
  North Vietnamese interests in, 85–86
  threat to, and Thailand, 70–71
Lin Piao, 21, 22, 23, 52
Lo Jui-ch'ing, 51

McCarthy, Senator Joseph, 3
Malaysia, 11, 18, 20, 39, 44
  Australian military assistance to, 65
  and British withdrawal from Singapore, 42–43
  economic development of, 45
  future US policies toward, 84, 88–89, 94, 96
Mao Tse-tung, 20, 23, 48–50, 53, 54, 79
  and Maoism, 22, 23
  military doctrine of, 51
Marcos, President Ferdinand, 37, 68
Marxism-Leninism, 20
Matsu, 75, 80
May, Ernest R., 31
Mekong River Development Project, 87, 91
Military Advisory Assistance Group (MAAG), 76
Mizo movement, 28, 29
Mozingo, David P., 22

Naga movement, 28, 29
National Liberation Front (NLF) of South Vietnam, 14, 16, 20
Nationalism, 13, 24, 44

Asian, 46, 102
nature of, 43
Nepal, 23, 27
New China News Agency, 23
Ne Win, General, 26, 27, 28
New Zealand, 11, 35
and British withdrawal from Singapore, 42–43
Japanese relations with, 60
US interests in, 36–37
US policies toward, 64–67, 96
Nonaggression pacts, 97
North Vietnam, see Democratic Republic of Vietnam
Nuclear Nonproliferation Treaty, 70, 82, 99
Nuclear Test Ban Agreement, 82

Overseas Economic Development Fund, 62

Pakistan, 32, 99
Paris Peace Talks, 7, 52
Pathet Lao, 10, 17, 25, 26, 71, 85
People's Liberation Army (PLA), 51, 52
Philippines, 11, 20, 32, 35, 44
economic development of the, 45
American relations with the, 68
future US policies toward the, 67–69, 94, 98
and Okinawa, 45
rebellion of the Hukbalahap in the, 68
Soviet relations with the, 59
US bases in the, 65, 68
US interest in the, 37
Polaris/Poseidon system, 45, 81

Quemoy, see Matsu

Red Guards, 48; see also Chinese People's Republic
Republic of China (ROC), 11, 35, 38, 39, 52–53
as Republic of Formosa, 76–80
future US policies toward the, 74–80
and Quemoy and Matsu problems, 75, 80
and Taiwan Strait, 53, 78
Thailand's relations with the, 73

US security obligation to the, 39
Republic of Korea (South Korea), 10, 11, 18, 35, 38
Communist control of, 36
US interest in, 36, 91

Salonga, Joirto, 67
Sihanouk, Prince Norodom, 17, 85, 86
Singapore, 11, 39
Australian military assistance to, 65
Barisan Socialists in, 88
British withdrawal from, 41, 42–43, 65, 99
future US policies toward, 84, 88–89, 94, 96
Japanese relations with, 62
Soviet relations with, 55, 58
Sino-Burmese Treaty of Friendship and Mutual Non-Aggression, 18n, 28
Southeast Asia
and ideology, 47, 102–3
and nationalism, 43–44
differences among nations in, 4
economic development of, 45–46
flexibility of nations in, 46
impact on, of US withdrawal from Vietnam, 29–30
and regionalism, 5, 44, 96–100
Southeast Asia Treaty Organization (SEATO), 2, 3, 4, 25, 42, 72, 84, 96, 99
South Vietnam, Government of (GVN), 8, 10
Soviet Union (USSR)
and US policy, 91, 93, 94
and détente with the US, 54, 59
in Southeast Asia, 22, 24, 27, 41, 57–60
relations with China, 52, 77, 80, 81

Taiwan, see Republic of China
Thai-Lao of northeast Thailand, 17
Thailand, 10, 11, 16, 17, 18, 20, 25, 35, 37, 43
and bilateral defense treaty with US, 70

China's interest in, 24, 25
and counterinsurgency, 72–73
economic development of, 45
future US policies toward, 69–74, 85, 91, 94, 98
and neutrality, 70
and regionalism, 44, 96
Soviet relations with, 70
US military and economic assistance to, 73–74
and US security planning, 69
Than Tun, 27
Thanat Khoman, 73n
Thanat-Rusk Statement (1962), 37, 69, 70, 71
Tri-Nation (US-UK-USSR) Security Council resolution, June 1968, 66, 69, 99
Truman Administration, 1, 2

United Nations
and future US policies, 73, 76, 79, 82
and postwar Vietnam, 87
United States
bases in Southeast Asia, 44, 65, 66, 68, 76, 81
——defense obligations, 63
treaties with Australia and New Zealand, 37, 64, 65
treaties with Japan, 36

treaties with Republic of China, 38, 75
treaties with Republic of Korea, 36
treaties with Philippines, 37
——foreign aid programs, 46
——national interests, 47, 101, 102
approaches to defining, 31–34
countries vital to, 35ff., 64ff.
countries not vital to, 39, 84ff.
critical elements of, 34–35
——see also Vietnam

Viet Cong, 8, 10, 13, 14, 16, 17, 18, 20–21
Viet Minh, 14, 15, 16
Vietnam
American involvement in, 7–8, 12
American withdrawal from, 9, 24, 29
and events of 1954, 1–5
see also Democratic Republic of Vietnam; South Vietnam

White Flag Communists, see Communist Party, of Burma
Wilson, Prime Minister Harold, 42
Wolf, Charles, Jr., 94
World Bank, 82

Zagoria, Donald S., 8